SQUADRONS!

No. 47

THE WESTLAND
WHIRLWIND

PHIL H. LISTEMANN

ISBN: 979-1096490-78-3

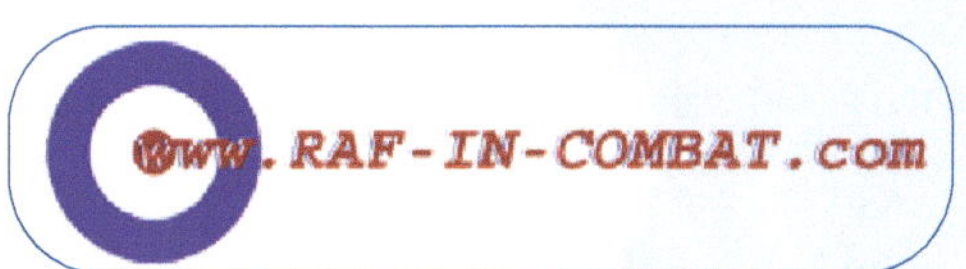

Colour profiles: Malcolm Laird

GLOSSARY OF TERMS

Personel :

(AUS)/RAF: Australian serving in the RAF
(BEL)/RAF: Belgian serving in the RAF
(CAN)/RAF: Canadian serving in the RAF
(CZ)/RAF: Czechoslovak serving in the RAF
(NFL)/RAF: Newfoundlander serving in the RAF
(NL)/RAF: Dutch serving in the RAF
(NZ)/RAF: New Zealander serving in the RAF
(POL)/RAF: Pole serving in the RAF
(RHO)/RAF: Rhodesian serving in the RAF
(SA)/RAF: South African serving in the RAF
(US)/RAF - RCAF : American serving in the RAF or RCAF

Ranks

G/C : Group Captain
W/C : Wing Commander
S/L : Squadron Leader
F/L : Flight Lieutenant
F/O : Flying Officer
P/O : Pilot Officer
W/O : Warrant Officer
F/Sgt : Flight Sergeant
Sgt : Sergeant
Cpl : Corporal
LAC : Leading Aircraftman

Other

ATA: Air Transport Auxiliary
CO : Commander
DFC : Distinguished Flying Cross
DFM : Distinguished Flying Medal
DSO : Distinguished Service Order
Eva. : Evaded
ORB : Operational Record Book
OTU : Operational Training Unit
PoW : Prisoner of War
PAF: Polish Air Force
RAF : Royal Air Force
RAAF : Royal Australian Air Force
RCAF : Royal Canadian Air Force
RNZAF : Royal New Zealand Air Force
SAAF : South African Air Force
s/d: Shot down
Sqn : Squadron
† : Killed

CODENAMES - OFFENSIVE OPERATIONS - FIGHTER COMMAND

CIRCUS:
Bombers heavily escorted by fighters, the purpose being to bring enemy fighters into combat.

RAMROD:
Bombers escorted by fighters, the primary aim being to destroy a target.

RANGER:
Large formation freelance intrusion over enemy territory with aim of wearing down enemy figthers.

RHUBARD:
Freelance fighter sortie against targets of opportunity.

ROADSTEAD:
Dive bombing and low level attacks on enemy ships at sea or in harbour

RODEO:
A fighter sweep without bombers.

SWEEP:
An offensive flight by fighters designed to draw up and clear the enemy from the sky.

The Westland **WHIRLWIND**

The Westland Whirlwind belongs to that category of aircraft which entered production but failed to live up to their designers' expectations. Its unreliable engines can be seen as a major reason for this but it only serves to hide other serious problems. Indeed, even with better engines the results would probably have been the same, as the concept of a twin-engine fighter aircraft capable of meeting single-engine fighters escorting bombers formations on an equal footing was fallacious, as combat in WW2 was soon to prove. Its American counterpart, the Lockheed P-38 Lightning, a far more powerful and superior fighter, was unable to contend with single-engine enemy fighters and after heavy losses had to relinquish this role to the P-47 and P-51. The P-38 was transferred to the role of fighter-bomber where it found a new lease of life. The Whirlwind was produced only in very small numbers but it too was soon withdrawn from pure interception duties.

In 1934 the Air Ministry launched a series of specifications aimed at providing a new monoplane fighter to replace the ageing biplanes then in RAF service. Indeed the expansion of the RAF, which had begun in 1935, was not simply concerned with increasing the numbers of aircraft in service but producing a number of new types of aircraft to equip the large number of newly formed squadrons and re-equip the ones already in service with RAF Fighter Command. Among the new specifications was the F.37/35 which called for a single-seat day and night fighter armed with cannons with a speed, rate of climb and ceiling well in excess of contemporary, and future bomber performances. Boulton Paul, Bristol, Hawker, Supermarine and Westland produced proposals to meet F.37/35 and eventually Westland won the competition with its P.9. Two prototypes, **L6844** and **L6845**, were ordered on 11 February 1937 against contract No.556965/36 and the type was soon named "Whirlwind". The first prototype was completed in late September 1938 and was an elegant twin-engined aircraft which looked more like a racer than a warplane. The Whirlwind introduced some advanced features, such as Fowler flaps, a new method using electron castings and magnesium alloy skinning. Initial ground handling and taxi trials began on 4 October 1938, and the first flight was made a few days later on the 11th, and fight testing began immediately.

From the beginning the Whirlwind was designed to be armed with four 20 mm cannons, a very powerful armament at that time. As a twin-engined fighter the armament could be concentrated in the nose of the aircraft giving an impressive concentration of fire power on targets, which were expected to be bombers, coming from the Continent.

However problems arose with the engines, Rolls-Royce Peregrines, which were experiencing recurrent overheating troubles. Also, with the new engineering and design concepts suffering from problems the Whirlwind's development programme began to expe-

A photograph of the first prototype, L6844, taken shortly before its first flight in October 1938. *(Phil Jarrett)*

Nice photographs of the first prototype showing its pure aerodynamic contours. The cockpit, with its all-round view, was one of the best features of the Whirlwind.
(Phil Jarrett)

rience delays. More problematical were its handling characteristics, including the lack of directional control, tail buffeting at the stall, and the ailerons which were considered to be too heavy. Meanwhile the RAE test programme continued but at a very slow level with only 25 hours of flying having been completed by April 1939. Worse was to follow as the number of modifications needed rose to 250! By that time the second prototype had made its first flight, on 29 March 1939, and joined the test programme. Nevertheless a confirmed order (contract No.980384/39) for 200 Whirlwind Mk.Is was placed and these received the serial numbers **P6966-P7015** (50), **P7035-P7064** (30), **P7089-P7128** (40), **P7158-P7177** (20), **P7192-P7221** (30) and **P7240-P7269** (30). A second contract (No.20186/39) for another 200 aircraft followed later in the year and these received serial numbers R4243-R4283 (41), R4296-R4325 (30), R4345-R4384 (40), R4400-R4445 (46), R4460-R4479 (20), R4499-R4521 (23).

Development testing continued during the summer of 1939 while the construction of the first production aircraft began, however the engines continued to be troublesome and eventually Royce-Rolls announced, in August 1939, the termination of the Peregrine and Vulture engine programmes to focus on the development of the Merlin which was showing great promise. Consequently the Air Ministry cancelled the second batch of Whirlwinds and reduced the first order to just 114 aircraft. A total of 116 Whirlwinds were built and the last was taken on charge in December 1941, equipping two fighter squadrons, Nos. 137 and 263. Both squadrons became later on fighter-bomber squadrons after the Whirlwind switched to this role. The type was eventually withdrawn from use in January 1944 and was replaced by the Hawker Typhoon.

A view of the each side of L6845, the second prototype. In this photograph the relatively large engine nacelles are clearly shown. While under construction L6845 incorporated some improvements and further modifications resulting from the testing of L6844. *(Phil Jarrett)*

September 1941
June 1943

Victories - confirmed or probable claims: 4.0

First operational sortie:
24.10.41
Last operational sortie:
21.06.43

Number of sorties: *ca.* 2,220
Total aircraft written-off: 30

Aircraft lost on operations: 22
Aircraft lost in accidents: 8

Squadron code letters:
SF

COMMANDING OFFICERS

S/L John SAMPLE (†)	AAF No. 90278	RAF	20.09.41	28.10.41
S/L Humphrey St.J COGHLAN	AAF No. 90117	RAF	01.11.41	20.05.43
S/L John B. WRAY	RAF No. 37874	RAF	20.05.43	…

SQUADRON USAGE

After a brief three-month existence in 1918 (when it had been formed to become a DH9-equipped bomber unit) No. 137 Squadron was scheduled to be re-form at Colerne, in No. 10 Group Fighter Command, on 20 September 1941. It was to become the second squadron to be fully equipped with the Westland Whirlwind. However, as it was due to replace No. 125 Squadron (Beaufighter VI), then based at Colerne's satellite, Charmy Down, this latter station became 137's birthplace.

By the end of September the new unit had 18 Whirlwinds on charge, but only three pilots; more were posted in, mainly from the first Whirlwind unit, No. 263 Squadron, so that by 19 October 1941, 137 Squadron was able to field one operational flight. The commanding officer, Squadron Leader J. Sample, had to convert to Whirlwinds, having flown Gladiators with No. 607 Squadron before commanding No. 504 Squadron, equipped with Hurricanes, throughout the Battle of Britain. Sample carried out the new unit's first operational sortie along with the South African Flying Officer C.A.G. Clark, flying to Predannack to undertake an attack on fuel containers which had been reported in railway sidings at Landerneau, inland from Brest on 24 October 1941. On arrival it was apparent that the fuel containers had been moved so the pilots attacked coal trucks and a locomotive.

'Johnny' Sample joined the Auxiliary Air Force in 1934 as a member of No. 607 (County of Durham) Squadron. By 1939 he was a flight commander and, with war approaching, was called up on 24 August. Still flying Gloster Gladiators, he took part in the only successful interception of an enemy aircraft to be made by UK-based Gladiators and shared in the destruction of a Do18 on 17 October. He moved to France with the squadron in November 1939 and participated in the Battle of France (now flying Hurricanes). On 10 May 1940 he was engaged in combat and made further claims (one shared probable -and two damaged aircraft) but was shot down, slightly injured and repatriated. Before the end of the month he had recovered and was given command of No. 504 (County of Nottingham) Squadron. He received the DFC in June. He flew in the Battle of Britain at the head of 504 and added more victories to bring his total to three confirmed (two shared), one shared probable victory, and two aircraft damaged. All of his claims made during the Battle of Britain were made on 15 September. In March 1941 he was posted for a rest and in September 1941 he was given command of 137 as it was forming. His command would be short however as on 28 October 1941, during a practice flight Sample's aircraft collided with another Whirlwind of the squadron and he was killed when his parachute failed to open completely.

Whirlwinds of No.137 Squadron lined up along the perimeter track at Matlask early in 1942. The nearest aircraft, SF-P, P6982, has earlier served with No.263 squadron; after accidental damage on 26 May 1942 it was repaired and stored at No.18 MU and scrapped in September 1944. (*CT Collection*)

After this tentative start to operations the Squadron received a most unfortunate setback when, during practice interceptions, Squadron Leader Sample's Whirlwind was in collision with another Whirlwind flown by a new pilot on 28 October. Sample's aircraft lost its tail unit, although the trainee landed safely. Sample tried to evacuate his aircraft but the parachute failed to open completely. Just two days later Flying Officer C.A.G. Clark, one of the Flight commanders and Sample's companion on the first operation, was forced to ditch in the Channel returning from another attack on Landerneau; although picked up by a destroyer, he died of his injuries. The Squadron was now declared non-operational, receiving 11 new pilots, all but one straight from No. 56 OTU with no twin-engine experience (an Oxford was duly allocated to the Squadron to provide the requisite training) while the new CO, S/L H. StJ Coghlan, posted from 263 Squadron arrived to command 137. On 8 November the Squadron moved to the east coast (RAF Coltishall) undertaking training flights and convoy patrols when the weather permitted. Two days later, another loss was recorded. A Spitfire and a Whirlwind took off at 12.10 to patrol base when after ten minutes, the pair was recalled due to very bad weather and low ceiling and Flight Sergeant B.L. Robertson crashed on landing. At the beginning of December 1941 the Squadron left the comfort of Coltishall for its less luxurious satellite, Matlask, which had been built the previous year. No. 137 Squadron's first contact with the Luftwaffe came on 3 January 1942 when a Ju88 was intercepted 30 miles off Cromer but, in what was to become an all too familiar scenario, the enemy aircraft escaped into cloud. Interceptions of reconnaissance Do217s took place on 1st and 5th February and although these aircraft were attacked they escaped with no results observed. The run of bad luck continued on 12 February 1942 when four Whirlwinds took off to carry out a convoy patrol but were unable to locate the Allied ships. However, two battleships were sighted and, believing them to be friendly, the Whirlwind pilots investigated; it was a fatal error. The ships were no less than the *Scharnhorst* and *Gneisenau* making their famous "Channel dash", with five or six destroyers and flak ships, and the Whirlwinds were immediately set upon by the Luftwaffe escort of 20 Bf109s. In the ensuing chaotic combat Pilot Officer J.L. DeHoux (RCAF) expended all his ammunition without apparent result and Canadian Flight Sergeant C.E. Mercer's guns frustratingly jammed with an enemy aircraft in his sights; although these two pilots returned safely Pilot Officer R.O.G. Häggberg, a Swede and Warrant Officer B.L. Robertson were not seen again. Two further pilots, Sgt A.W. Sandy, at the eve to receive his commission and P/O G.W. Martin took off to carry out the same patrol some 30 minutes after the first formation, also failed to return. All four were apparently shot down by the Bf109s.

March and April 1942 passed with fruitless scrambles to investigate suspected "tracks", and uneventful convoy patrols, but some deadly accident were recorded. On 9 March, P/O C.W. De-Shane (RCAF) was killed when he spun off during practice dogfight with a Spitfire and two months later another Canadian lost his life, P/O R.E.D. Wright, when one of the wing broke off during aerobatics. On 8 May 1942 six aircraft were detached to Coltishall operate at night against an expected raid on Norwich. A Do217 was seen but the Whirlwind pilot was not in position to attack. On 15 May 1942 however, Flight Sergeants J.R. Brennan and A.G. Brunet, both Canadians, intercepted a Ju88 and the former pilot claimed strikes before the Ju88 disappeared into cloud. His aircraft was hit by return fire and landed at Coltishall on one engine. It seemed No.137 Squadron's luck had changed on 27 May 1942 when Brennan

and Pilot Officer P.M. La Gette reported intercepting a Ju88 which, after attacks from both pilots, crashed in the sea 20 miles off Cromer. However, a Coastal Command Blenheim was last plotted at the same location and it is likely this was the "Ju88". Brennan was last seen heading east after the combat, reporting "everything under control" but was not seen alive again. Two days later, 137 lost another Whirlwind after an engine failure during the return flight from an early morning patrol. The pilot, P/O D. St.J Jowitt was forced to bale out over Sherington when his left engine caught fire at 800 feet; the Whirlwind went into a spin thereafter. Another frustrating combat took place on 20 June 1942 when Warrant Officer C.E. Mercer and Flight Sergeant J.H. Ashton (both RCAF) were scrambled in the evening and sighted a Do217 crossing their path 2,000 yards ahead, some 30 or 40 miles east of Great Yarmouth. The Do217 dived to sea level and the Whirlwinds gave chase. Ashton made two attacks and Mercer expended all his ammunition, noting at least 3 or 4 strikes, but the Dornier made good its escape. The last week of June was marked by another of a Whirlwind caused by an engine which caught fire on flight on the 27th. The pilot, P/O F.M. Furber, a Rhodesian who was on an evening patrol, had to abandon his aircraft over Sheringham. July 1942 seemed to be going the same way when on the 6th another Ju88 escaped, albeit damaged, but the 25th of the month saw 137 Squadron's first confirmed victory. Two Whirlwinds were patrolling a convoy off Smiths Knoll in the early evening, Warrant Officer R.L. Smith spotted an unidentified aircraft approaching at sea level. As the aircraft, a mile distant and identified as a Ju88, turned away, the Whirlwinds gave chase and, with the advantage of height and a shallow dive, quickly closed to firing range. In fact the lead Whirlwind flown by Canadian Pilot Officer J.E. McClure overshot and as he turned away to reposition fire from the Ju88's dorsal turret hit the Whirlwind's starboard engine. Smith was positioned astern and having missed with his first burst from 500 yards, closed to 250 yards expending all his ammunition, seeing strikes on the starboard engine. Throttling back, McClure came in again from astern and slightly starboard, opening fire with a 2-second burst at 100 yards, closing to 50 yards. At that range the effect of the Whirlwind's four closely-grouped 20mm cannon must have been devastating and as McClure broke away he saw flames from the fuselage and more strikes on the starboard engine. The Ju88 started to climb but McClure closed in again with a four-second burst closing to 25 yards. The Ju88 stalled and dived straight into the sea. It seemed now that 137 had the bit well and truly between its teeth, as the very next day two Ju88s and Do217 were intercepted during three separate sorties, but the Ju88s employed their low-level performance to escape and the Dornier, attacked at night, evaded whilst the Whirlwind pilot, Sergeant F.G. Waldron, was blinded by cannon flash. However, on the 29th of the same month another Ju88 fell to Squadron's guns when Flight Sergeant J.R. Rebbetoy (RCAF), and Sergeant H.L. O'Neill were vectored from their evening convoy patrol to intercept the hostile aircraft. In heavy mist, the Ju88 was not seen until it was 200 yards away, giving the German pilot no time to evade. Both pilots expended all their ammunition in several attacks but the Junkers flew on for another 15 miles before its bombs were jettisoned and it crashed into the sea with starboard wing ablaze.

At the beginning of August the Squadron flew to Drem, east of Edinburgh to take part in an Army exercise *Dryshod*. The units role was taken over temporarily by No. 266 Squadron who flew their Hawker Typhoons into Matlask from Duxford. Two days before 137 Squadron returned, 266 Squadron demonstrated the new fighter's low-level performance by catching and destroying one of the elusive Ju88s, the first Typhoon victory. A brief flurry of interceptions in mid-August, which resulted in a Do217 destroyed and three further Ju88s damaged brought to an end this chapter of Squadron's history, as on 24 August 1942 the Squadron moved inland to Snailwell, north-east of Cambridge, where, it was informed its main duties would be night flying. Accordingly most of September was spent on night-flying training and from 12th of the month, bombing practice, as the Whirlwinds were now being equipped to carry a 250- or 500-lb bomb under each wing. The only operation flown was a Rodeo on 3 September 1942 in which No. 137 Squadron were escorted by 24 Spitfires from Nos. 411 (RCAF) and 485 (NZ) Squadrons and 36 Typhoons of the Duxford Wing (Nos. 56, 266 and 609 Squadrons). This impressive force swept over Belgium to Dixmude but no enemy reaction was forthcoming. The Squadron moved to Manston, the nearest base to Occupied Europe on 17 September 1942, a move which promised rather more contact with the enemy. The rest of the month, however, was spent in more bombing and night flying practice. Operations started again in October, with local patrols and shipping recces. This was the period when Luftwaffe fighter-bomber attacks on the south coast intensified and on 25 October 1942 the new A Flight commander, Flight Lieutenant J.W.E. Holmes and Sergeant H.L. O'Neill attempted to intercept four Fw190s, but were unable to close or prevent them bombing Dungeness. Three days later Air Marshal Leigh-Mallory visited to brief the Squadron on its role at Manston; night-flying seemed to be forgotten and 137 Squadron would be used on Rhubarbs and similar operations. These began disastrously on 31 October when three of four

Whirlwind pilots of 137 Sqn photographed at Manston on 5 March 1943. Left to right, F/O R.L.Smith, F/O E.L. Musgrave (RAAF, †18.05.43), P/O D.A. Roberts (RNZAF), Sgt J.McG. Barclay (†31.07.43), W/O A.G. Brunet (RCAF), F/L J.M. Bryan (†10.06.44 as W/C Flying 136 Wing), F/O J.L. Dehoux (RCAF, †02.09.43), Sgt A.C. Smith (PoW 01.04.45 with 193 Sqn), F/O A.C.McClure (RCAF), P/O N. Dugdale, Sgt T.A. Sutherland, Sgt E.A. Bolster, F/O J.M. Hadow (†15.04.43), S/L H.StJ.Coghlan, F/Sgt H.L.O'Neill (†12.07.45 with No. 110 Sqn), F/Sgt R. Woodhouse. Behind, Whirlwind P7002/SF-W which was lost on 4 April 1943. (*CT Collection*).

Whirlwinds that set out for Le Touquet failed to return. All fell victim to flak with one pilot taken prisoner, Sgt F.G. Waldron, and two ditching in the Channel, only one of whom, F/L J.E. van Schaick, was rescued. Pilot Officer D. St.J. Jowitt was posted missing. In the afternoon of the same day six Whirlwinds intercepted a Fw190 near Margate but, as if to emphasise the harsh environment in which they were now operating, despite the Whirlwinds 'clocking' 300 mph, the German fighter pulled away with ease. During November the night flying practice was put to good use when Intruder sorties were added to 137 Squadron's repertoire, the main targets being the railway systems. The location of the airfield meant engagements with the Luftwaffe could happen any time and on 19 December 1942 Flying Officer J.M. Bryan and Pilot Officer J.R. Rebbetoy (RCAF) on practice 'cloud flying' sighted two Fw190s which they promptly attacked; after a dogfight in which both Whirlwind pilots got in bursts, the Fw190s turned for home, one streaming black smoke was last seen diving on its side from about 400 feet. The 137 Squadron pilots were credited with a probable. Later, on the 22ⁿᵈ, Sgt T.A. Sutherland took off at 11.25 for Rhubarb operation around Abbeville (France) with F/O E. Musgrave (RAAF) who was leading. They found a goods train stationed at a small station and both dropped their 250-lb bombs on it. At that moment Sutherland was hit by flak that was coming from each side of the station. Suffering strikes in the starboard engine and through the port cowling he set course to base. However one engine seized before the English coast was reached and he crash-landed at Lympne. If 1942 ended with a loss, 1943 didn't started in a better way with three losses recorded in January, the first on the evening of the 17ᵗʰ. Pilot Officer J.F. Luing took off at 01.22 from Ford with another pilot for an intruder operation. While taking off his Whirlwind hit a hole causing a wing-tip to touch the ground. The aircraft caught fire, and 'Jack' Luing was able to escape from it before the bombs exploded. A few days later, W/O A.I. Doing and Sgt A.E. Brown were both shot down by flak while attacking ground targets in France; only W/O Doing survived as a PoW. With the loss of P7061 in a flying accident on the 13ᵗʰ, whose pilot survived, January had been far to be a good month. At the end of that month however, the first decoration received by a pilot of the Squadron was awarded, a DFC to Pilot Officer R.L. Smith (who already had a DFM) for his work on Blenheim before joining 137 Squadron and for destroying (with McClure) a Ju88 and attacking four Fw190 single-handed, as well as undertaking a number of successful Rhubarbs. The Squadron was now flying a mix of shipping patrols, Rhubarbs and Intruders, with mounting success. By 6 February 1943, Flying Officer Bryan had attacked and damaged 12 trains; ten days later he would be promoted to command A Flight. On 10 February 1943 Pilot Officer E.L. Musgrave (RAAF) attacked a 5000-ton motor vessel at night, off Boulogne; despite accurate defensive fire he dropped two 250 lb bombs which must have hit home as the vessel stopped for more than an hour and then took shelter in Boulogne Harbour. His aircraft was hit in the elevator and shrapnel pierced the canopy but he returned safely. The 18 February 1943 brought a record 16 sorties in a night but with terrible price. Two pilots were lost

Above and below, spring 1943, Whirlwind P7012/SF-V being re-armed at Manston for another bombing mission over the Occupied Europe.

when a Whirlwind taking-off collided with another taxying and bombs exploded. Among the two pilots, Lt N.A. Freeman, one of the few SAAF pilots seconding the RAF in Europe. On 2 March, three Whirlwinds took off 13.10, S/L Coghan leading, to attack railways targets in the Neufchatel area. The trio were forced to return after making a brief landfall as cloud-base was down to hilltop level. Warrant Officer A. Brunet (RCAF) lost Sgt G.O.H. Walker in cloud, who asked for a vector home. Walker indicated that he was Ok but when Brunet was near the English coast he heard the former give a Mayday, which was not picked up by the ground station. Searches were made by Brunet, P/O 'Jack' Luing and W/O 'Ash' Ashton (RCAF), with no success. Walker was later reported PoW at *Stalag* 344. The 5 March 1943 brought a visit from the press in which Flight Lieutenant Bryan performed the required "beat-up" in SF-A. A week later he received a DFC for work with the Squadron, his score now stood at a Do217 destroyed, a Fw190 probably destroyed and 20 trains damaged. On 14 March 1943 six Whirlwinds attacked Abbeville with 250-lb bombs, escorted by Spitfires of Nos. 350 (Belgian) and 453 (RAAF) Squadrons as close cover and Nos. 64 and 122

Squadrons as top cover. Bomb bursts were seen on NE side of aerodrome. At the end of the month the Squadron carried out satisfactory trials with 500-lb bombs. Throughout the spring of 1943, 137 Squadron carried on its war on enemy shipping in the Channel. When operating by day it was now usually escorted, sometimes by Spitfires but more often by the Typhoons of the Manston-resident Nos. 198 and 609 Squadrons. At night, and by May most of the sorties were at night, single Whirlwinds attacked E-boats, R-boats and minesweepers in the Channel or the adjacent ports, or dropped bombs on marshalling yards or Luftwaffe airfields, notably Poix which received several visits. But losses were high. In the last three months of operations, four Whirlwinds were lost in operations, costing the lives of F/O J.R. Rebbetoy (RCAF) on 25 April and F/O E.L. Musgrave (RAAF) on 15 May. In the same period of time, three more Whirlwinds were wrecked in three different accident, one of them being fatal to P/O J.M. Hadow on 15 April.

The Squadron was now due for re-equipment, and Typhoons were confidently expected; the new CO, Squadron Leader J.B. Wray, arranged for his pilots to get some unofficial Typhoon time with No.609 Squadron - with whom they shared the airfield. However, there was a desperate shortage of Typhoons due to the lack of serviceable Sabre engines and re-equipment with the type was postponed. Apparently 137 Squadron was due to receive Vultee Vengeance dive-bombers at one stage but this was changed to Hurricane IVs. The Squadron flew to Southend on 12 June 1943 and their Hurricanes began to arrive three days later. Whirlwind operations continued for a short while, the last sorties being flown on the night of 21 June 1943 when Poix was again the target, this time receiving 500-lb bombs, possibly their only operational use on Whirlwinds of the Squadron; the pilots were Squadron Leader J.B. Wray (P7096), Flight Lieutenant J.M. Bryan (P7047), Flying Officer J.F. Luing (P7046) and Warrant Officer J.H. Ahston (RCAF).

Claims - 137 Squadron (Confirmed and Probable)

Date	Pilot	SN	Origin	Type	Serial	Code	Nb	Cat.
25.07.42	P/O John E. **McClure**	Can./ J.15505	RCAF	Ju88	**P7104**	SF-V	0.5	C
	W/O Robert L. **Smith**	RAF No. 742902	RAF		**P7012**		0.5	C
29.07.42	F/Sgt James R. **Rebbetoy**	Can./ R.75651	RCAF	Ju88	**P7058**	SF-G	0.5	C
	Sgt Leo **O'Neill**	RAF No. 530323	RAF		**P7005**	SF-H	0.5	C
19.08.42	F/O John M. **Bryan**	RAF No. 102570	RAF	Do217	**P7121**	SF-C	0.5	C
	Sgt Desmond A. **Roberts**	NZ411994	RNZAF		**P7046**		0.5	C
19.12.42	F/O John M. **Bryan**	RAF No. 102570	RAF	Fw190	**P7114**		0.5	C
	P/O James R. **Rebbetoy**	Can./ J.15741	RCAF		**P7005**	SF-H	0.5	C

Total: 4.0

Date	Pilot	S/N	Origin	Serial	Code	Fate
30.10.41	F/O Colin A.G. **CLARK**	RAF No. 42192	(SA)/RAF	**P7091**		†
10.11.41	F/Sgt Basil L. **ROBERTSON**	RAF No. 748333	RAF	**P6977**		-
12.02.42	P/O Ralph O.G. **HÄGGBERG**	RAF No. 120677	(SWE)/RAF	**P7093**	SF-A	†
	W/O Basil L. **ROBERTSON**	RAF No. 748333	RAF	**P7107**		†
	Sgt John A.W. **SANDY**	RAF No. 1051978	RAF	**P7050**		†
	P/O George W. **MARTIN**	RAF No. 102619	RAF	**P7106**	SF-D	†
27.05.42	F/Sgt John R. **BRENNAN**	CAN./ R.72637	RCAF	**P7122**		†
29.05.42	P/O Douglas St-J. **JOWITT**	RAF No. 114169	RAF	**P7118**	SF-O	-
27.06.42	P/O Frederick M. **FURBER**	RAF No. 80203	(SR)/RAF	**P7049**		-
31.10.42	F/L John E. **VAN SCHAICK**	RAF No. 114086	RAF	**P7064**	SF-G	-
	Sgt Francis G. **WALDRON**	RAF No. 1277168	RAF	**P7109**	SF-N	**PoW**
	P/O Douglas St-J. **JOWITT**	RAF No. 114169	RAF	**P7115**		†
22.12.42	Sgt Thomas A. **SUTHERLAND**	RAF No. 655932	RAF	**P6998**		-
17.01.43	P/O John F. **LUING**	RAF No. 121527	RAF	**P7051**		-
23.01.43	W/O Alec I. **DOIG**	RAF No. 565057	RAF	**P7054**		**PoW**
	Sgt Alfred E. **BROWN**	RAF No. 646417	RAF	**P7095**	SF-H	**PoW**
19.02.43	P/O Charles E. **MERCER**	CAN./ J.15738	RCAF	**P7114**		†
	Lt Neville A. **FREEMAN**	SAAF No. 19862	SAAF	**P7119**	SF-W	†
02.03.43	Sgt George O.H. **WALKER**	RAF No. 1382117	RAF	**P7005**	SF-H	**PoW**
04.04.43	P/O Norbury **DUGDALE**	RAF No. 131147	RAF	**P7002**	SF-W	-
25.04.43	F/O James R. **REBBETOY**	CAN./ J.15741	RCAF	**P7058**	SF-G	†
17.05.43	F/O Edward L. **MUSGRAVE**	AUS. 403528	RAAF	**P7063**		†

Total: 22

Date	Pilot	S/N	Origin	Serial	Code	Fate
28.10.41	S/L John **SAMPLE**	AAF No. 90378	RAF	**P7053**		†
09.03.42	P/O Charles W. **DE-SHANE**	CAN./ J.15148	RCAF	**P7036**	SF-X	†
04.05.42	P/O Robert E.D. **WRIGHT**	CAN./ J.15147	RCAF	**P7103**		†
30.06.42	*Ground accident*	-	-	**P7101**	SF-A	-
13.01.43	Sgt Edmund A. **BOLSTER**	RAF No. 1090706	RAF	**P7061**	SF-P	-
30.03.43	P/O John T. **DAVIDSON**	RAF No. 114577	RAF	**P7104**	SF-V	-
15.04.43	P/O John M. **HADOW**	RAF No. 122121	RAF	**P7121**	SF-C	†
01.05.43	Sgt Aubrey C. **SMITH**	RAF No. 1340628	RAF	**P6976**	SF-X	-

Total: 8

A brunch of Canadian pilots:
L-R, front row: Sgt C.W. De-Shane (†09.03.42), Sgt J.L. DeHoux (†02.09.43), Sgt J.H. Ahston.
Back row: F/Sgt J.R. Rebbetoy (†25.04.43) P/O J.C. Lawton, the only British on this photo (†15.10.42 with 51 OTU), Sgt C.E. Mercer (†19.02.43), F/Sgt A.G. Brunet.
(CT collection)

Various nationalities served 137 and among the most represented were the South Africans. Below left, F/O A.G.C. Clark from Johannesburg who joined the RAF just before the war. Initially posted to 266 Sqn in December 1940, he was posted to the FIU in June 1940 and with which he participated to the Battle of Britain. In September 1941 he was posted to 263 and soon after to 137 and served the squadron until to be killed on 30.10.41. Below in the middle, Lt N.A. Freeman of the SAAF, who belonged to a group of SAAF pilots sent at the end of 1941 to second the RAF and killed with Sgt C.E. Mercer on 19.02.43 (see above). Below right, Sgt R.P.G. Häggberg, one of the few Swedes who enlisted in the RAF during the war. It was because he was schooled in England that he could enlist as early as October 1939. He was one of the four 137's pilots killed on the fateful day of 12 February 1942.
(CT and R. Bowater collection)

Victories - confirmed or probable claims: 7.0

First operational sortie:
07.12.40

Last operational sortie:
29.11.43

Number of sorties: *ca.* 3,350

Total aircraft written-off: 57

Aircraft lost on operations: 32
Aircraft lost in accidents: 25

Squadron code letters:
HE

COMMANDING OFFICERS

S/L Henry EELES	RAF No. 26177	RAF	...	17.12.40
S/L John G. MUNRO	RAF No. 36016	RAF	17.12.40	18.02.41
S/L Arthur H. DONALDSON	RAF No. 34150	RAF	18.02.41	22.08.41
S/L Thomas P. PUGH	RAF No. 40137	RAF	22.08.41	12.02.42
S/L Robert S. WOODWARD (†)	RAF No. 74698	RAF	12.02.42	07.12.42
S/L Geoffrey B. WARNES	RAF No. 78429	RAF	08.12.42	15.06.43
S/L Ernest R. BAKER	RAF No. 40660	RAF	15.06.43	...

SQUADRON USAGE

The first unit selected to operate the Whirlwind was No.25 Squadron, a night fighter unit, so far equipped with Blenheim Mk.Is. In May, the Squadron received two Whirlwinds for evaluation as night fighters, but the experiment was short-live and the Squadron was converted to Beaufighter instead. But that was a false start. On 10 June 1940, two days after the loss of HMS *Glorious* 263 Squadron was reformed at Drem, Scotland. It was the first squadron to receive the RAF's latest fighter the twin engine Westland Whirlwind. Production problems with the Peregrine engines led to a delay so a number of Hurricanes were issued to the squadron as a stop gap measure. The first Whirlwind, P6966, reached the squadron on 6 July 1940. This aircraft was flown in by the Squadron's new commander, Squadron H. Eeles. A week later another two arrived but the very next day one of them was damaged in a forced landing. As expected with new aircraft there were a number of problems with the engines and the airframe.

Henry Eeles entered RAF College as a regular officer in January 1929 and one year later was appointed to a Permanent Commission. He first served with No. 41 Squadron and was then posted to the Middle East. He returned to the UK in 1934 and went to the Air Armament School to attend a course. Thereafter, he served in various staff positions and had reached the rank of Squadron Leader when war broke out in September 1939. At the end of June 1940, with the need of fighter pilots, he was sent to No. 6 OTU for a refresher and conversion course on Hurricanes. The next month, he took command of No. 263 Squadron which was flying Hurricanes while waiting to convert to the Whirlwind. He brought 263 to operational status and left the squadron in December 1940. No more operational positions followed and he ended the war with the rank of Air Commodore. Eeles continued his career in the RAF until retiring as an Air Commodore in January 1959. *(Tom Eeles)*

F/L D.A. Crooks (A Flight CO), a Canadian from Toronto, S/L J.G. Munro (CO) and F/L T.P. Pugh (B Flight CO), January 1941.
John Munro joined the RAF with a direct-entry commission in September 1934. This was one of the few offered in competition each year to graduates of British and Commonwealth universities (Cambridge in Munro's case). Upon completing his training, he was posted to No. 47 Squadron at Khartoum (Sudan). He returned to the UK in February 1936 and was posted to the Aircraft Armament Co-operation Flight. Later, in 1937, Munro went to the Air Armament School and moved to Research and Development in the Air Ministry in August 1938 where he was associated with the design of servo-fed 20mm cannons (later installed in RAF fighters). He maintained in this position until being sent to No. 5 OTU in June 1940 for a refresher course and conversion to Hurricanes. He was posted to No. 263 Squadron as a Squadron Leader in mid-July 1940 but was immediately detached to the Air Ministry. Returning to the squadron three weeks later, his knowledge of 20mm cannons helped the Whirlwind, which was equipped with four such guns and new to the RAF, to become operational by the end of the year. In December 1940 he eventually took command of the squadron and led it until mid-February 1941 when he went to the Aircraft Gun Mounting Establishment as Chief Test Pilot and Chief Technical Officer. Munro then spent the rest of war in various RAF technical positions and finally in a series of staff jobs in the UK and India from July 1943 onwards as a Wing Commander. Munro served in the RAF until 1949 and retired as a Group Captain. Crooks and Pugh did not survive the war. *(Westland Archives)*

In addition the four 20mm cannon were prone to jamming. The Whirlwinds were formed into C Flight under the command of Flight Lieutenant W.O.L. Smith, the other flights flying Hurricanes. This flight was to develop the Whirlwind and iron out any of its bugs. As with the previous month training continued with most days seeing aircraft in the air. Pilots were still familiarising themselves on the Whirlwind, although C Flight still remained non-operational. Training continued to be the norm for most days. The Whirlwind flight was eventually disbanded and the Squadron reverted back to the normal two flights. A Flight became the developing flight with the Whirlwinds, B flight keeping its Hurricanes. On 7 August 1940 the first Whirlwind P6966 was lost. During take-off Pilot Officer I.F. McDermot, a Canadian serving in the RAF, suffered a burst tyre. Informed that the undercarriage had suffered damage he baled out near Stirling. The Squadron moved to Drem on the South side of the Firth of Forth on 2 September 1940. Here they were in an ideal position to defend the naval base at Rosyth. While day and night patrols were flown by the Hurricanes, A Flight was still non-operational and the pilots continued to work up on the Whirlwind. Continuing delays in engine production meant that by October the squadron only had eight Whirlwinds on strength. In mock combats with the Hurricanes the Whirlwind proved to be superior in speed at low level and made the Hurricane look too slow. In November the Squadron gave up its Hurricanes and the Whirlwinds moved to Exeter. The Squadrons' first operational patrol was carried out on 3 December 1940 under the command of Squadron Leader Eeles. Eeles was posted to Drem on the 16th and Squadron Leader J.G. Munro took over as the new CO. In an effort to make some use of the new Whirlwinds one flight from No. 263 Squadron was posted to St Eval on the Cornish coast. During January 1941 the Squadron still maintained a detachment at St Eval. During Luftwaffe raids on South Wales and the South East of England E-Boats were stationed off the coast to act as rescue boats in case any enemy aircraft came down in the sea. It was decided to try and engage these boats as they returned to their French base. These were given the code name *Chameleon*. Three such patrols were carried out on the 9th, 13th and 17th but no E-Boats were encountered but in the meantime on the 12th 263 sustained its first fatality on Whirlwind when F/O A.W.N. Britton was killed during an air-sea firing exercice; he was seen diving into the ea off Burnham. The St Eval detachment carried out a number of scrambles to intercept enemy aircraft. Most were unsuccessful but on the 12th Pilot Officer D. Stein caught a Ju88 40m South West of the Scillies. After his initial attack the Junkers was

Whirlwind P6969/HE-V in which P/O K.A.G. Graham claimed the first Whirlwind confirmed 'kill' on 8 February 1941, a Ar196 float plane.

Three Whirlwinds, P6969/HE-V, P6985/HE-J and P6987/HE-L flying in formation at the beginning of 1941. None survived the war.

last seen in a spiral dive and as the Whirlwind was not carrying a camera gun, P/O Stein could only claim it as damaged. After investigation, Fighter Command would upgrade this claim to a confirmed victory at the end of February. In the meantime, 263 was looking for its first official success. On 13 January, F/O R.J. Hugues and Sgt C.P. Rudland saw an enemy aircraft thirty miles off the Lizrad but were unable to catch it, whilst on the 19th P/O P.G. Thornton-Brown and P/O H.H. Kitchener caught a He111 twenty miles south of Land's End and chased it out passed the Scillies before breaking off short of fuel. The same day, F/L T.P. Pugh was victim of a rare accident when he experienced a double engine failure during a test flight and he was forced to abandon the Whirlwind over Middlemore. Finally, the first official success at the time for the squadron came on 8 February. During a patrol an Arado Ar196A-4 was attacked and shot down by Pilot Officer K.A.G. Graham. During this engagement Graham was also shot down and killed by the return fire from the rear gunner. The rest of the month was pretty quiet with the bulk of operations being flown from the St Eval detachment. At the end of the month it was decided to send the rest of the squadron to St Eval so the unit could now operate as a whole. Squadron Leader Munro was out and his place was taken over by Squadron Leader A.H. Donaldson, the brother of Squadron Leader J.W. Donaldson who commanded the Squadron in Norway. During a patrol off the Cornish coast on 1 March 1941 Pilot Officer P.G. Thornton-Brown damaged a Ju88. Pilot Officer Thornton-Brown was in action again on the 5th. He and Pilot Officer Kitchener damaged another Ju88 off the Scillies Isles. These actions were not always all one sided however. On the 11th Pilot Officer

Arthur Donaldson belongs to a sibling of three brothers who became all a Companion of the DSO while commanding a fighter squadron in WW2. His brothers were John William (†08.06.40 as OC 263 Sqn) and Edward Mortlock. Arthur Donaldson joined the RAF in 1934 and his first assignment was 56 Sqn upon completion of his training. During the first months of the war, he served as a flying instructor. In January 1941, he went to 56 OTU for a refresher course and then posted to 242 Sqn as supernumerary squadron leader and was posted the following month to command 263 Sqn. He opened his score on 1 April by damaging a Do17. Other claims followed and in September he was awarded the DFC. He stayed with the unit until August 1942, then sailed to Malta when he became WingCo Flying of the Takali Wing. In this position, he made his final claims, the very last one on 14 October, to bring his total to five confirmed victories (two shared), two probables (one shared) and five aircraft damaged. However, during his last engagement, he was wounded in both feet and lost two fingers on his left hand. He left Malta two weeks later bound for Gibraltar. As the Liberator was coming in to land, it crashed and ended up in the sea. He was rescued and eventually made it back to the UK. He was awarded a DSO in November and a Bar to his DFC in December, but no further operational flying positions were held before the end of the war. He remained in the RAF and retired in March 1959.

Two Whirlwinds, coded HE-Z and HE-S taking-off from St Eval in 1941 for another patrol *(CT Collection)*

H.H. Kitchener was severely injured when he was hit by return fire from a Ju88 off the Cornish coast at 1710hrs. He crash-landed his damaged aircraft which was destroyed in the subsequent fire. Three days later on 14 March 1941, Pilot Officer P.G. Thornton-Brown crashed at Portreath while returning from a convoy patrol and seriously injured. On 18 March the whole squadron moved to Portreath and for the remainder of the month the Squadron took part in numerous convoy patrols. On the first day of April Squadron Leader Donaldson and Flight Lieutenant D.A.C. Crooks, a Canadian serving in the RAF, intercepted a Do215 5 miles north of Predannack and claimed it as damaged. Flight Lieutenant Crooks failed to return and it was thought he was shot down by the rear gunner. Flying Officer B. Howe and Pilot Officer A. Tooth came across one He111s on 6 April which was claimed as damaged. The next day a lone raider was tracked near Falmouth and Flying Officer R.F. Ferdinand and Sergeant C.P. King were scrambled to intercept. They came across a Ju88 to the South of Falmouth and after a brief engagement it escaped into cloud, but with no result. Another move occurred in April, this time back to Filton. Flying Officer B. Howe died on 20 April 1941 as a result of an accident near Wittering airfield. His Whirlwind broke up in the air after a part became detached from the airframe. Another pilot was lost on the 30th; Pilot Officer G.S. Milligan was undertaking mock attacks on a Wellington when his Whirlwind broke up in the air and crashed. These two losses may have been the result of the wing leading edge slats breaking off during tight turns. Other similar incidents occurred and as a result a decision was taken to lock the slats in place. This had no detrimental effect on the aircraft's performance.

During 1941 Fighter Command started to carry out sweeps over occupied Europe. At first there were two types of sweeps, *Rhubarbs* and *Circuses*. A Rhubarb was carried out solely by fighters. A *Circus* was carried out by a small number of bombers with a large escort of fighters. The idea was to entice the Luftwaffe up into the air where the RAF fighters would be waiting for them. It was decided not to risk the Whirlwinds on these operations as they were thought to be too vulnerable, much in the same way as the Bf110s were, when operated over England. However it was decided to try them on *Warheads*, which were low level attacks on enemy airfields. The Whirlwinds were also to take part in *Mandolins*, which were unescorted fighter attacks on enemy airfields. During May the Squadron was involved in 81 convoy patrols and about a dozen scrambles. No enemy aircraft were encountered but one Whirlwind was lost by accident, on the 29th, when Sgt D.F.J. Tebbit wrote off an aircraft after a collision with a balloon cable during a training flight; he crash-landed the Whirlwind two miles north of Chepstow and the aircraft was destroyed in the subsequent fire. The convoy patrols continued into June and during the month 67 patrols were carried out with a further 7 scrambles involving a total of 152 sorties. Two pilots were lost during the second week, both by accident, Sergeant R.G. Pascoe on the 11th and the next day Pilot Officer R.F. Ferdinand, both being killed. The Squadron took part in their first offensive operation on 14th. *Warhead* 1 was a double sweep against Querqueville and Maupertus airfields. Squadron Leader Donaldson and Pilot Officer Rudland carried out the sweep against Querqueville. On the way out over the coast a lighthouse was also damaged. Squadron Leader Donaldson was hit in the port engine nacelle but he managed to get back to base safely. The second sweep was flown by Flight Lieutenant T.P. Pugh and Pilot Officer D.W. Mason against Maupertus airfield. Here the target was covered in mist and so the attack was cancelled. July was another quiet month for the squadron with convoy patrols being the norm. The first week of August was a busy one for the Squadron. On the 4th 263 carried out its second *Warhead* and again it was a double operation. Squadron Leader A.H. Donaldson and Flight Lieutenant J.G. Hughes attacked Querqueville airfield. Both Whirlwinds were damaged during the attack. Flight Lieutenant T.P. Pugh and Pilot Officer D.W. Mason carried out an attack on Maupertus airfield. On the way home Mason attacked an E-Boat ¼ mile North of Cherbourg. It was left in a sinking condition, which Mason claimed as sunk. *Warhead* 3, another 2-part operation, was carried out the next day. Squadron Leader A.H. Donaldson and Sergeant J.W.E. Holmes attacked Maupertus airfield. Both pilots strafed Ju87s and Bf109s claiming one Ju87 destroyed on the ground with two more Ju87s and two Bf109s as damaged. Two lorries, one with troops in, were also shot up. The second patrol was a shipping recce of Cherbourg by Flight Lieutenant Hughes and Sergeant D.St. Jowitt. No shipping was seen but a wireless station was shot up. The Squadron returned to Maupertus on 6 August with *Warhead* 5. Pilot Officer C.P. Rudland claimed one Ju87 destroyed on the ground and fired a two second burst at a Bf109 just as it left the ground, seing it catch fire and crash. Two more Ju87s were claimed destroyed on the ground, while two more plus two Bf109s were claimed as damaged. On the run out over the coast two tankers were encountered and both of these were damaged. Later that same day *Warhead* 6 was put into motion. This was to locate and destroy the two tankers that were previously damaged in the earlier raid. Although the tankers were not found the four Whirlwinds encountered a number of Bf109s and a general dogfight took place between 1,500 feet abd sea level. Pilot Officer C.P. Rudland claimed one of the Bf109s shot down, while another was claimed by Flight Sergeant R.A. Brackley. Squadron Leader A.H. Donaldson claimed a third as damaged. The Squadron also carried out the occasional escort mission. On the 12th the Whirlwinds escorted 54 Blenheims on their way to Cologne during Operation 77, although the Whirlwinds only went as far as Antwerp. On the return journey the squadron attacked a number of vessels. One flak barge was sunk and another damaged. A new change of command took place on the 22nd, when F/L P.T. Pugh became the new CO. Operations continued and lannion airfield was the target on the 24th. Newly promoted Wing Commander A.H. Donaldson led Flight Lieutenant P.T. Pugh, Pilot Officer C.P. Rudland and Sergeant A.V. Albertini on a sweep over the airfield. A RDF station and a navigation beacon were damaged. On the return flight nine Bf109s were spotted but they refused to enter combat. Another 2-part operation took place on the 26th. Maupertus airfield was attacked and five Ju87s claimed destroyed on the ground. During an attack on Lannion airfield five Ju88s were claimed destroyed. *Mandolin* 3 was carried out against Lannion airfield on the 29th. Flight Lieutenant J.G. Hughes and Sergeant J.W.E. Holmes damaged a RDF station and a blockhouse. On the last day of the month 263 took part in *Gudgeon* 4 a cover for returning Blenheims that had attacked Lannion

263 Sqn pilots in February 1942 at Colerne.
Front row: F/Sgt J.P. Coyne (RCAF), F/Sgt H.D. Muirhead (RCAF, †17.02.43 with 401 Sqn), Sgt K.C. Ridley, P/O J.J. Walker (†23.07.42), Sgt D.F. Small (†09.11.42 in a flying accident as a passenger in a Defiant), F/O S.J. Lovell (†29.01.44 with 183 Sqn), F/Sgt W.A. Lovell (American serving in the RCAF, †11.02.44 with 1st FS, USAAF).
Second row: F/Sgt E. Brearley (RCAF, †09.09.42), P/O J.W.E. Holmes, P/O N.V. Crabtree (American serving in the RCAF), S/L T.P. Pugh (CO, †02.08.43 as OC 182 Sqn), G/C Harvey (Station CO), F/O G.B. Warnes (†22.02.44 as OC 263 Sqn), F/O E.C. Owens (Adj), P/O P. Harvey (Irish), P/O H.J. Blackshaw (†15.05.43).
Third row: P/O A.A. Hay (EO), Sgt P.A. Ewing (RAAF, PoW on 15.09.42 with 450 Sqn), P/O V.L. Currie (†23.07.42), P/O S.G. Brannigan (RNZAF, †11.08.42 with 501 Sqn), F/Sgt C.P. King (West Indian, †18.04.43), Sgt D.R. Gill (RCAF, †07.11.42), Sgt C.D. Bell (Australian serving in the RAF, †11.09.44 127 Sqn).
Back row: F/Sgt R.I. Reed (American serving in the RCAF, †20.02.44 with 4th FG, USAAF), Sgt B.C. Abrams (South African serving in the RAF, †18.04.43), F/Sgt I.F. Kennedy (RCAF), F/Sgt P.A. Jardine (South African serving in the RAF, †21.09.42), Sgt W.R. Wright (South African serving in the RAF). *(C. Goss Collection)*

airfield. Twelve Whirlwinds took part in another Gudgeon operation on 4 September 1941. A formation of six Blenheims had raided Cherbourg Harbour when six Bf109s were encountered. In the dogfight that followed Sergeant G.L. Brackwell was shot down baled out off Cherbourg and was taken prisoner. Blenheim escort was again the order of the day on the 8th. A convoy had been sighted near Alderney and 11 Whirlwinds provided escort. As well as providing escort the Whirlwinds were to be used for flak suppression. The results were rather good with one 400t vessel left on fire, one tug sunk and two tugs and three barges damaged. The presence of the Luftwaffe was discovered very late when Sergeant King, some miles north of Ardeney, saw tracers passing his machine. He took evasive action and saw a Bf109 about 500 yards behind. He managed to shake it off, but on landing several bullet holes were found in his machine. Two days later early on the 10th two Whirlwinds set off to attack the Gestapo HQ at Quineville. Poor visibility hampered the mission and as they crossed the coast one of them piloted by Pilot Officer D.W. Mason was hit by flak from a gun position and crashed. Flying Officer D. Stein then carried out four attacks on the gun position and silenced it. Another Mandolin was laid on for Lannion airfield the next day. The attack in the late evening left one Ju88 destroyed and two dispersal pens damaged. As the formation neared Plymouth Sergeant T. Hunter experienced problems and baled out 5 miles from the coast. His body was not recovered. Flying Officer H. Coghlan ran out of fuel and crashlanded during his approach to land at Predannack, but the damages were superficial. In September No. 137 Squadron was re-formed to become the second Whirlwind squadron and a large number of pilots and ground personnel were posted from the Squadron to 137. With the posting of so many experienced pilots an influx of new pilots fresh from OTUs arrived during October. A period of intense training soon followed and as a result there was very little operational flying, apart from two missions at the end of the month. During a practise flight on the 9th two Whirlwinds collided. Flight Lieutenant H. Coghlan was able to bale out but Pilot Officer O.J.H. Hoskins was killed. An attack on the airfield at Morlaix was scheduled for the 29th. Two pilots, Flight Sergeant R.A. Brackley and Sergeant C.P.King took off from Predannack at 1445hrs. They attacked from the south and Brackley claimed a Ju88 as damaged. King fired a burst at a hanger, which was observed to be hit; he then fired at a Ju88 but failed to notice any damage. King collided with a mast, which damaged his port coolant tank. As King headed for home he shot up a gun post on the way. Shutting down the overheated engine King was able to cross the coast and land back at base okay. Another two-man strike was laid on for Morlaix again the next day. Flying Officer D. Stein and Sergeant K.C. Ridley took off at 0945hrs. The airfield defences were ready and Sergeant Ridley was hit by flak but managed to get back to base, although he ran off the runway. Flying Officer D. Stein was not so lucky and he failed to return. It was first thought he may have survived and taken captive but it was later learned that he had been killed. During early November Flight Lieutenant Coghlan was promoted to Squadron Leader and posted to take command of No. 137 Squadron. On 6 November 1941 *Rhubarb* 56 was carried out near the Cherbourg Peninsula. No shipping seen and the section set course back to base but Sergeant J.J. Robinson appeared to dip one wing into the sea and crash. He was presumed killed. Another Rhubarb took place the next day to recce distillery targets. The object was to locate various distilleries for future targets. A number of Bf109s were encountered and Sergeant C.P. King from the West Indies, claimed one shot down. While he was ready to attack goods train, he saw two Bf109s on his his right beam at the same height. One enemy aircraft turned to attack him and fired at extreme range. King turned at zero feet to the right and climbed towards to cloud cover, eventually reaching 5,000 feet. His Whilrwind out-climbed the Bf109 and he then flew northwards on a zigzag course for about ten minutes. Cloud cover now diminished and he could see that his position was about three miles west of Cape de la Hague. At this moment, he saw again two Bf109s on his right beam about 300 feet above him. Both enemy aircraft turned to the left diving to beam attack on the right side. King dived slightly and turned to the right keeping underneath them, then, as one of the Bf109 turned to the right again, he was able to pull up and fire a one and a half second burst at him from 150 yards, suing full deflection. There was an explosion like a ball of flame at the back of the cockpit and it went into a very steep dive with black smoke and flames pouring from it. On his side, Flying Officer G.B.Warnes was also attacked by two Bf109s but he was able to evade them by doing steep turns at sea level. During early December a move was made from Filton to Charmy Down and another death was recorded when Sergeant D.E. Prior was killed on 14th. He was participating in a search light co-operation exercise when his aircraft, was seen to crash near Coleford. The rest of the month was quiet with no encounters with the enemy.

January 1942 was a very quiet month for the Squadron due to the bad weather, which curtailed most flying but one Whirlwind stricken from inventory when it caught fire on the ground and burnt out on 3 January. In the middle of the month 263 moved to Colerne. Training in air-to-air firing and practise attacks both with and without camera guns were carried out whenever the weather permitted. On 5 January 1942 it was announced that all fighter squadrons should become operational at night as well as during the day.

Whirlwind P6991/HE-R seen at dispersal in March 1942. This aircraft eventually crash-landed on 9 February 1943 with Sgt J. Macauley in command. He escaped without scratches. *(Phil Jarrett Collection)*

Two days later Pilot Officer H.J. Blackshaw and Sergeant W.Lovell were scrambled after two 'bandits' (later identified as Bf109s) that were reported between Plymouth and Ibsley. One of these (Bf109E-7 W.Nr4970) suffered engine failure and the pilot, *Unteroffizier* Kurt Thüne from 1./(F)123 baled out and was captured near Bovey Tracey. February brought another move for the Squadron, this time to Fairwood Common in Glamorganshire on the 10th. On 12 February 1942 Squadron Leader T.P. Pugh was posted from the squadron as Squadron Leader Tactics to HQ No.82 Group. His place was taken over by Squadron Leader R.S. Woodward who came from No. 137 Squadron. The runways at Fairwood Common were not really suitable for the Whirlwinds and as a result a number of accidents occurred. On 13 February Pilot Officer J.P. Coyne (RCAF) was injured after his Whirlwind, P7108 swung on landing and overturned, but the aircraft was repaired. Between the 19th and 21st problems also arose with the Peregrine engines, which resulted in a temporary grounding of all aircraft in late February. The defect was traced to faulty three way unions, which supply oil to the camshaft and supercharger bearings. Stronger unions were supplied by Westlands and fitted to all Whirlwinds. The flying ban was lifted on 4 March and training resumed. Three days later on the 7th Sergeant P.A. Jardine, a South African serving in the RAF, suffered a heavy landing. He hit the ground hard and burst both tyres, causing the Whirlwind to overturn. Jardine survived the accident but suffered spinal injuries, but the aircraft would be struck off charge in June and one week later, P/O V.L. Currie burst a tyre on landing and the undercarriage collapsed; the Whirlwind was not repaired. Convoy patrols continued and on 25 March the Whirlwind was presented to the press and public for the first time. The Whirlwind was no longer a secret. Another Whirlwind was lost on 1 April when Pilot Officer P. Harvey was coming into land. He was hit by a 50mph crosswind and bounced on landing. The Whirlwind turned over and disintegrated. Harvey was able to walk away from the wreckage with little more than a bruised arm. The next day Sergeant B.C. Abrams, another South African serving in the RAF, suffered from hydraulic failure and collided with a fuel bowser and he hit a dispersal pen; the Whirlwind did not survive the crash. On 18 April the squadron moved to Angle. Convoy patrols were still the norm. On the 27th Flight Lieutenant C.P. Rudland was ordered up to shot down a loose barrage balloon. Although he only had ball ammunition the balloon went up in flames. Three days later a Ramrod was carried out to Morlaix airfield, although bad weather prevented the target from being attacked and no attack could be made. During May the Squadron was heavily committed to convoy patrols. The Squadron flew a total of 535 hours and 55 minutes on operational flights and 282 hours and 40 minutes of non-operational flights. No accidents of any kind were reported, surely a record for the Squadron if not Fighter Command. Several scrambles took place but no interceptions took place. On 5 June 1942 the Squadron recommenced Rhubarb operations. Four Whirlwinds took off from Predannack at 1513hrs to attack Lannion airfield. Squadron Leader R.S.Woodward attacked a row of five Ju88s. As he completed his attacked he noticed that they looked like dummies. Pilot Officer J.P. Coyne (RCAF) also recognised the Ju88s as dummies after he had attacked them. Pilot Officer H.J. Blackshaw also saw the dummy Junkers and avoided them. He did however spot a Ju88 being serviced in a hanger and opened fire scoring a number of hits. Flight Sergeant H.D. Muirhead achieved hits on two blister hangers in the northern part of the airfield.

Plans were in hand to equip the Whirlwinds with bombs. Trials were carried out in July 1942 when one aircraft was fitted with two Mk III universal bomb racks outboard of the engine nacelles. At first 250-lb bombs were fitted but later 500-lb were tested. The 500-lb bombs put a strain on the wings and so only 250-lb bombs were to be used. A simple push button release was fitted near the throttle levers. A jettison switch was also fitted. These modified aircraft became known as Whirlibombers. During a dive these bomb-laden aircraft had a tendency to drop the port wing, plus pilots were advised to drop both bombs at once. If they dropped them singly then it was advised to drop the port one first. Although still based at Angle, B Flight was detached to Portreath from 1 to 8 July 1942. Convoy patrols and scrambles were the routine for the squadron. It wasn't until the end of the month that they saw any real action. At 1534hrs on the 23rd Squadron Leader R.S. Woodward led twelve Whirlwinds from their advance based at Predannack. As they approached the Lizard at 300ft they met up with their escort from No. 234 Squadron. Squadron Leader Woodward and Pilot Officer Coyne (RCAF) attacked railway trucks at Landivisiau Station. They then flew back to Predannack via Morlaix where they shot up some trucks. As they crossed the Channel Coyne attacked two vessels and saw strikes on one of them. Here they joined up with four other Whirlwinds and set course for home. They spotted one Whirlwind being followed by two Bf109s. Before they could intervene the Whirlwind was shot down. As they neared the coast they saw another Whirlwind being pursued by three more Bf109s. Although Woodward turned back he did not see the aircraft again. In the meantime, Flight Sergeant C.P. King (West Indian) and Pilot Officer V.L. Currie attacked a truck near Morlaix but Pilot Officer Currie was last seen with four other Whirlwinds near the French coast. It may have been Currie that was shot down over the sea by the Bf109s. Pilot Officer J.J. Walker and Sergeant B.C. Abrams (South African) flew south to Landivisiau and turned towards St Tregonnec. A train was attacked in Belair Station and hits were registered but Pilot Officer Walker failed to return from this attack. Flight Lieutenant G.B. Warnes and Pilot Officer S. J. Lovell attacked a number of targets to the north of a railway line between Landivisiau and Landerneau and Pilot Officer J.W.E. Holmes and Sergeant W.R. Wright, a South African serving in the RAF, attacked the same targets as Green Section plus the same target that was attacked by White Section while Flight Lieutenant C.P. Rudland and Pilot Officer P. Harvey were able to fire on three railway trucks coming out of St Pol de Leon. One truck was left glowing red. At the end this mission gave globally satisfaction even if two pilots were lost. Sorties continued the following weeks. On 18 August 1942 the Squadron moved from Angle to Colerne. There was very little in the way of flying during the month. The maintenance crews worked very hard at fitting all aircraft with bomb racks and by the end of the month this had been completed. A number of enemy shipping was reported in the Channel Islands area on 4 September. As the Squadron was the only operational fighter-bomber Squadron

In the summer of 1942, the Whirlwind became a fighter-bomber. Here seen at its dispersal at Warmwell, one Whirlwind, loaded with bombs is waiting for its pilot for a next mission. *(C. Goss Collection)*

Above, a bomb rack installed under the wing of Whirlwind P7062/HE-L, a rack able to carry a single 250-lb bomb, a 500-lb being too streesful for the wing. Left one of the bomb racks receiving its bomb.
(C. Goss Collection)

within No. 10 Group four of the Whirlwinds were sent to RAF Bolt Head. From here they carried out two Roadstead operations in the Channel Islands area but failed to find any enemy shipping. It was however the first operation on which Whirlwinds were fitted with bombs. Eight Whirlwinds led by Squadron Leader R.S. Woodward took off on an anti shipping strike in the Alderney - Cap de la Hague area on the 9th. Four large armed trawlers were found and in the resulting attack two of them were claimed sunk. These ships involved were the coasters *Henca* (305t) and *Tinda* (280t) escorted by VP207 and VP209 of the 2.*Verpostenflotille*. During the attack the *Henca* was hit by one bomb, causing it to capsize and sink in seven minutes. VP207 was hit and damaged, with two crew killed and seventeen injured. The first attack with bombs was a clear success. Three days later the rest of the Squadron moved to Warmwell. To help relieve other squadrons or when RAF Zeal was non-operational the Whirlwinds undertook other types of sorties including Air Sea Rescue flights off the Channel Islands. On 21 September 1942 Sergeant P.A. Jardine (South Africa) was lost when his Whirlwind dived into the ground near Dorset. Also, night flying practise was carried out on the night of 23/24 September. It was hoped that as many pilots as possible would be operational at night in order to carry out night operations. The rest of the month was pretty quiet and although number of operations took place nothing of importance was noted. In October less than 40 sorties were carried out but two more Whirlwinds were lost, one during an operation when F/L A.N.W. Johnstone crashed on take off on the 8th and one during a practice flight on the 28th when F/L J.R. Cooksey was obliged to land with the undercarriage retracted. Both pilots escaped without injuries. On 7 November 1942 Pilot Officer D.R. Gill (RCAF) led four Whirlwinds on a Rhubarb sortie. After bombing a railway line Gill disappeared and failed to return. It is thought he may have been shot down by flak. Pilot Officer E. Brearley (RCAF) and Sergeant F.W. Yates (Irish) carried out a successful *Rhubarb* on the 16th; a number of railway lines were destroyed and on the return journey Sergeant Yates attacked and damaged an E-Boat. The remainder of the month continued with Rhubards, Roadsteads and shipping recce's missions but very little was encountered either due to a lack of targets or poor wea-

ther. The next major event took place on 7 December 1942 when a number of Whirlwinds participated to an anti-shipping strike to the Channel Islands. A small force of German ships, were spotted 10km to the South of Jersey. Coming into attack Warrant Officer D.B. McPhail (RCAF) was hit by a hail of AA fire from one of the ships and he crashed into the sea. Squadron Leader R.S. Woodward was also shot down and killed, a great loss for the Squadron. But

Whirlwind P7043/HE-A was usually flown by F/L G.B. Warnes during the autumn 1942 but it was lost on 7 November that year with P/O D.R. Gill on board. *(J. Brewer)*

four of the ships were claimed as sunk or seriously damaged. One of these ships may have been the *Kronwijk* (622t), which was lost off Jersey on this day. The next day Flight Lieutenant G.B. Warnes was promoted to Squadron Leader and posted to command the Squadron to replace S/L Woodward. In the afternoon of the 14th two Whirlwinds flown by J.P. Coyne (RCAF) and M.T. Cotton (RAAF) carried out a sweep to the north of Barfluer. They failed to spot any suitable targets and set course for home. They were roughly 30km north of Cherbourg when they met and engaged two Fw190s from 10./JG2, which were returning from a raid on Swanage. Both Coyne and Cotton fired at the Fw190s but could only claim one as damaged. Both Whirlwinds returned undamaged but dangerously low on fuel. Flying for the remainder of the year consisted of practise flying, shooting and bombing.

The start of the New Year was very quiet for 263. Although numerous convoy patrols and Rhubarbs were carried out no major successes were reported. February was more busy. On 9 February, Sgt J. Macauley saw his right engine to fail whilst taking-off for a practice flight; he avoided high tensions cables but hit a tree and crash-landed in a field. The aircraft was good for scrap. Three days later, 12 February 1943 Flying Officer P. Harvey (Irish) and Sergeant D.J. Williams took from Warmwell for a Rhubarb. They crossed the coast near Cap de Carteret and just inland the spotted two goods trains. Harvey attacked one and saw strikes form his cannon hit the engine. Williams may have attacked the other train but his Whirlwind was hit by flak and headed for the coast. As he crossed the coast he sank lower towards the water until he eventually crashed into the sea 4m off Cap de Caterat. Harvey circled the area and saw Williams in the water trying to get into his dinghy. After a couple of orbits he headed for home. As soon as he landed he was off again to lead an air sea rescue Walrus from No. 276 Squadron to pick up Williams. When they reached the area the sea was too rough for the Walrus to land so reluctantly he set course back to base. Williams was posted missing. An Army co-operation exercise was held on 19 February 1943. Whirlwinds carried out a number of dummy attacks on army transport to give them an idea of what it was like to be attacked from the air. During one such attack Flight Sergeant F.L. Hicks (RAAF) hit a tree and his Whirlwind cartwheeled into the ground and exploded, killing the pilot. During early March, A Flight and the Squadron HQ was based at Harrowbeer, while B Flight was at Fairwood Common. The early part of the month was taken up with convoy patrols and the occasional dusk patrol. March was close to be a free-accident month until the 30th when P/O J.T. Davidson crashed the Whirlwind he was piloting after the left engine failed in flight. Roadstead operations were the main course for the first two weeks in April, although very little in the way of targets was found. On the 14th during *Roadstead* 52 to the West of Brest Sergeant J.

A few 263 Sqn pilots in the spring of 1943.
From left to right : Sgt J.I.Simpson (†09.10.43), F/Sgt K.C. Ridley, Sgt D.F.J. Tebbitt, F/L H.J. Blackshaw, A Flight CO (killed a few days later, 15.05.43), F/L J.W.E. Holmes, B Flight CO recently posted back from 137 Sqn, the Canadian Pilot Officer J.P. Coyne, and the CO, Squadron Leader G.B. Warnes (†22.02.44 as OC 263).
(C. Goss Collection)

'Reg' Baker joined the RAF in May 1938. He joined 210 Sqn flying Short Sunderlands, and when war broke out developed a highly successful strategy for attacking U-Boats, sinking three and earning him his first DFC in November 1940. In the autumn of 1941 he attended a Specialist Navigation Course in Canada and returned to 210 Sqn now flying Catalina's. In May 1942 he was posted to India to join 240 Sqn, but en-route crash-landed in Malta. Declared unfit to fly with Operational Stress, he was grounded for 8 months. Converting to fighters in late 1942, he then joined 182 Sqn flying Hawker Typhoons in a ground attack role until June 1943. Promoted to Squadron Leader, he was posted to command 263 Sqn and in October 1943 was awarded his second DFC for a daring low level attack on the German Ore Carrier '*Munsterland*' in bad visibility in Cherbourg Harbour, scoring a direct hit. Promoted to Wing Commander in April 1944 he became the Wing Leader of the 146 Airfield (later Wing from 12 May 1944), flying Typhoons and leading the Wing on many successful raids over Northern France, both before and after D-Day. It was on 16th June 1944 that his good luck eventually ran out whilst leading an attack on German positions holding three important River Bridges. After being hit by intense flak, his Typhoon dived towards the ground, crashing in an orchard at St-Mauvieu in Normandy. He was awarded the DSO the day of his death.
(CT Collection)

Macauley failed to return. Two days later, during a night Rhubarb on the 16-17th Flying Officer E. Brearley (RCAF) was lost in the Isigney area. His body was later washed ashore at Swanage. The bad sequence continued and the Squadron suffered a heavy blow on another sortie during the next night. During a shipping recce from the Channel Islands to Caen Flying Officer P. Harvey and Flying Officer C.P. King failed to return while the same night during another shipping recce to Cabourg Flying Officer B.C. Abrams also failed to return. The Squadron exacted some revenge on the 27th. Squadron Leader G.B.Warnes led six Whirlwinds on a shipping recce just South of Jersey. Here they spotted a convoy of nine ships. A barge was probably sunk and one ship estimated at 1,500t was set on fire plus an armed trawler was seriously damaged. Two other ships, including an E-Boat were shot up. No Whirlwinds were lost during this operation. Another convoy was located and attacked the next day. Pilot Officer M.T. Cotton (RAAF) received a flak hit to his right wing but he returned to base without any further mishap. This convoy was subject to another attack the following day. One of the escort vessels was sunk during this attack. After this short period of intense operations the number of serviceable Whirlwinds had dropped to a low level. It was getting rather difficult to replace the losses, as no aircraft were available from either Westlands or the Maintenance Units that provided back up aircraft. Also the number of qualified pilots to fly the night sorties was well below the required number to maintain the squadron at an operational level. Therefore the squadron was put on a 30-minute readiness level only. The number of sorties passed from 120 in April to 92 in May. As with previous months the first fortnight of May was without any major success. This changed on 15 May 1943, although it also saw the loss of a pilot. During a night shipping recce Flying Officer A. Lee-White (from Peru of British parentage) bombed a 2,500t ship and saw a large explosion. Later Squadron Leader G.B. Warnes, F/L H.J. Blackshaw, F/L J.W.E. Holmes and Sgt J.I. Simpson attacked a convoy at Barfleur. During the return flight Blackshaw was seen to orbit Exeter and Harrowbeer. His aircraft then dived into the ground and exploded, killing the pilot. During a shipping recce carried out the next day two Fw190s were engaged by the Whirlwinds. Flying Officers A. Lee-White and J.P. Coyne (RCAF) managed to obtain strikes on both enemy aircraft but they broke off and escaped any further damage. The Whirlwinds still carried their two 250lb during this engagement. A large convoy action took place on the night of the 21-22nd. Squadron Leader G.B. Warnes led four other pilots to an area between Cap de la Hague and Cherbourg. Warnes bombed a 3,500t vessel and stayed near the convoy to direct the attacks of the other pilots. Holmes and Cotton bombed the same vessel as Warnes. Coyne bombed and sank one of the escorting trawlers. As Flying Officer Lee-White came into attack his starboard engine was hit by *flak* and it burst into flames. He continued his attack on one of the trawlers. As he prepared to bale out the flames died down and he decided to head back to base. The engine started to burn again but he landed back at Warmwell safely. The 23rd saw four Whirlwinds, Flight Lieutenant Holmes, F/Sgt K.C. Ridley, F/O J.P. Coyne (RCAF) and P/O P.T. Cotton (RAAF), took off for an anti-shipping strike near Guernsey. The fighter-bombers had an escort of Spitfires from the Ibsley Wing. On coming through the Russel Strait they spotted a line of seven ships near St Peters Port. Coming in on a North-South run the pilots braved the murderous flak that was thrown up from the ships. As the pilots dropped their bombs they were unable to observe much damage due to the intense flak, although the bombs dropped by F/L J.W.F. Holmes were seen to explode on the mid-section of one coaster. It was later reported that the ship, an ex-Dutch coaster *Oost Vlaanderen*, 421t sank. In return Cotton's Whirlwind was hit by accurate 20mm flak and holed in the right wing fuel tank. On return the aircraft was inspected and subsequently struck off charge as being unrepairable. Again the number of serviceable aircraft in the squadron was giving cause for concern. On 29 May 1943 it was announced that No. 137 Squadron was being re-equipped with Hurricanes. Their Whirlwinds were transferred to No. 263 Squadron, which brought their serviceable number up to around 20. A number of 137 Squadron pilots were also posted into the squadron. A very few number of sorties were carried out in June, but that was enough to see another Whirlwind lost in action. On 15 June 1943 Pilot Officer Cotton (RAAF) was shot down by flak after dropping his bombs on a minesweeper. During this attack on a convoy to the north east of Sark an M Class minesweeper, M483 was sunk, possibly by Flying Officer A. Lee-White. Flight Sergeant G.A. Wood's Whirlwind, P7110 was also hit by flak in the tail and rudder. The day also saw the arrival of Squadron Leader E.R. Baker to take over command of the Squadron. Due to an increased influx of

263 Squadron 25 July 1943 at Warmwell.
L-R back: Sgts W.A. Handley and P.F. Cooper.
Next row : Sgts Kelly and Cole (both groundcrew), F/Sgt J.G. Hughes, F/L K.J.F. Funnel (†24.12.43), P/O R.C. Hunter (†22.02.44), F/Sgt G.A. Wood, F/Sgt R.C. Beaumont (†18.08.44 with 84 GSU), F/Sgt I.D.MacD. Dunlop, Sgts Armstrong and Harvey (both groundcrew), Sgt D.C.Todd, Sgt Rogers (groundcrew).
Sitting: W/O D.F.J. Tebbitt (PoW 22.02.45 with 41 Sqn), F/O J.E. Holman, F/L D.G. Ross (†05.06.44 as OC 198 Sqn), F/O P.R. Green (M.O.), F/Sgt Williams (groundcrew), F/L J.P. Coyne (RCAF), S/L E.R. Baker (Squadron's CO, †16.06.44 as Wing Leader of 146 Wing), F/L J.E. McClure (RCAF), F/L E.C. Owens (Adj), F/O D.E.G. Mogg (†26.12.43), F/O O.Ash (E.O.), F/O A.S. Wordsworth (I.O.).
Sitting front: Sgts G. Williams (†13.02.44) and W.E. Watkins, F/Sgt J.I. Simpson (†09.10.43), Sgt H.M. Proctor (†24.08.44).
(C. Goss Collection)

new pilots the Squadron moved to Zeals, Wiltshire for a period of intensive training. By this time the squadron was down to just 10 serviceable aircraft. On 12 July 1943 the Squadron moved back to Warmwell, Dorset to begin operations across the Channel, but once more, few ops were flown. On the 13th returning from a practice flight, Sergeant L.J. Knott was coming in to land when he stalled from 50-80ft and crashed short of the airfield. The Whirlwind, P7110 was destroyed but Knott was safe. That was to be the main event of the month because the four recce patrols carried out on the 13th, 18th, 20th and 23rd no major action was encountered, other than flak. The rest of July was very quiet. Another accident was recorded on 1 August 1943, Sergeant C.P. Cooper bounced on landing and crashed. Cooper was slightly injured but the Whirlwind was a write off. During the 11th a strike was laid on after a number of E-Boats were reported in the estuary of Abervrach. Squadron Leader Baker led six other Whirlwinds on the strike. An escort was provided by Spitfires from No. 302 (Polish) Squadron, which were to provide flak suppression. Coming in at low-level the Spitfires went in first. As the Whirlwinds came in they selected their targets and dropped their bombs. Squadron Leader Bakers bombs were seen to hit one E-boat, which blew up. Altogether four E-boats and one trawler were claimed to have blown up from direct hits, while one E-boat was left in flames. *Flak* was reported as very light from the E-Boats but heavy from the shore. The only damage to the Whirlwinds was one bullet in the engine nacelle of one fighter. The E-boats that were attacked were from the 4th and 5th E-boat Flotillas. The War Diary for the unit states that on 11 August 1943 20-25 fighters and fighter-bombers attacked E-Boats moored in l'Abervrach. E-boat S-121 was hit by bombs and set on fire. The ammunition then exploded and the E-Boat sank. Two other E-Boats, S-84 and S-136 received damage to their hulls and engines due to machine guns, cannons and bomb splinters. They were out of action for two weeks while undergoing repairs. S-117, possibly from the 4th Flotilla was also heavily damaged. Squadron Leader E.R. Baker carried out a night recce of the Channel Islands on the 14th. He came across a lone E-Boat and dropped his bombs on it causing an explosion. A little later, while of Guernsey he saw a He111 1000 yards ahead and 200 feet above him, flying on a parallel course. He climbed and closed slowly from below and 10° off to avoid being seen and then fired a short burst from 200 yards dead astern. The enemy aircraft's left engine caught fire and another burst sent the He111 crashing into the sea; it was the last claim made by a pilot of Whirlwind during the war. The next night the squadron undertook a recce over Cherbourg harbour. Squadron Leader E.R. Barker dropped his bombs on an armed trawler, which was last seen in a sinking condition. This may have

Operation *Starkey*, end of summer of 1943. The Whirlwinds of 263 are being prepared, all painted with white and black stripes around the wings and a white nose. Below P6974/HE-M with this special markings, the same aircraft is in the forefront on the photo above. *(Westland Archives)*

been the ex-Dutch *Iris* of 200t, which was sunk at Cherbourg by aircraft on 15 August 1943. From the next and for the next three weeks, 263 participated to Operation *Starkey*.

Operation *Starkey* took place between 16 August and 9 September 1943. It was basically a ruse to lure the Germans into believing the Allies were going to invade France near Boulogne. It was also intended to divert valuable German resources from the Eastern Front. The operation involved mainly British and Canadian forces with the added help from the United States Army Air Force. The British Second Army was deployed to the Dover, Folkstone and Newhaven area while the Canadian First Army moved into the Portsmouth and Southampton area. The operation was split into three phases; the Preliminary Phase 16 to 24 August, Preparatory Phase 25 August to 7 September and the Culminating Phase 8 to 9 September. The role of the air forces was to bomb nearby airfields, railways, industrial and other targets of opportunity. The Whirlwinds of No. 263 Squadron took part in two operations on the 8 and 9 September. For these operations the Squadron moved to Manston airfield and came under the command of No. 11 Group. Aircraft that took part in this operation were given black and white stripes on the wings. Twin-engine aircraft also had their noses painted white. This applied to the Whirlwinds. During this period, one Whirlwind was damaged by the CO on 10 September, when the aircraft hit a ridge while landing at Warmwell and the left undercarriage broke off. Operation *Starkey* was followed by Operation *Chattanooga Choo-Choo* commenced on 17 September. This operation was devised by Squadron Leader Baker in co-operation with No. 10 Group Intelligence. The aim of the operation was to sever the main Rennes-Brest railway line between Lamballe and Morlaix. If the railway could be severed then the stranded trains should be easy targets for the roving Whirlwinds and Mosquitoes. More missions were carried out until the end of the month and 263 performed 80 sorties in September. However, the Squadron sustained one loss during a strike on Morlaix airfield on the 23rd (*Ramrod* 85), Flight Sergeant G. Wood who was shot down by ground fire over the aerodrome. But he managed to evade capture and returned to the UK with help from the Resistance. In October, the number of sorties remained stable. During the early evening of 8 October Squadron Leader E.R. Baker successfully bombed an E-Boat off Varriville. He landed back at base at 2025hrs. Two hours later two pilots landed back and reported that they had shot up a 2,500t flak ship. Immediately Squadron Leader Baker organised a strike on the ship. On arrival in the target area the ship was located and attacked. Flak was very heavy from Alderney and Cap de la Hague as well as the flak-ship. A sea haze was also making it difficult to locate the target and there was an increased risk of collision. Squadron Leader Baker ordered the formation to return to base. On their return they were informed that Warmwell was covered in fog and to land at Tangmere. Pilot Officer J.I. Simpson suffered engine failure and as he came in to land at Tangmere the other engine failed as well. He crashed 100 yards short of the runway and was killed when he hit an anti-landing post.These train busting sorties continued. Two trains were damaged by Pilot Officer H.M. Proctor and Flight Sergeant I.D.M. Dunlop on the 19th. In the afternoon of the same day Pilot Officer N.P. Blacklock and Sergeant R.C. Beaumont hit a goods train near Airel. On landing back at base Pilot Officer Blacklock overshot and in order to prevent a major crash, raised the landing gear and bellied in. On the 24th, 263 participated to *Roadstead* 79, a low-level

Group of 263 Sqn NCO pilots in the summer of 1943.
From left to right : Sgt R.J. Hughes, Sgt J.B. Purkis, Sgt H.M. Proctor (†24.08.44), F/Sgt R.C. Beaumont (†18.08.44 with 84 GSU), Sgt L.S. Gray (PoW 24.10.43), F/Sgt K.C. Ridley. *(C. Goss Collection)*

P6971 was one of the last operational Whirlwinds still in use at the end of 1943. It served with 263 Sqn in 1941, carrying out 11 operational sorties that year. It served briefly with 137 Sqn between September and December 1942 but no operational flights were recorded. It eventually arrived at 263 Sqn at the end of December 1942 where it carried out 26 more operational flights. Its last operational take-off occurred on 26 November 1943 with Flight Sergeant Ian Dunlop at the controls.
(C. Goss Collection)

attack on Cherbourg harbour. The main target was the MV *Münsterland*, a 6,400 tons ship, a blockade runner carrying a cargo of rubber, wolframite and nickel, large enough to supply two divisions for two years. Flak was intense and terrifying...The eight Whirlwinds which were involved in this attack were hit and two would be unable to return base. Flight Sergeant L.S. Gray was shot down and captured. Flying Officer P.T.R. Mercer's aircraft was hit by flak twice and he crashed into the sea. Flight Lieutenant D.G. Ross was hit in the right wing and he carried out a belly landing at Warmwell. The Whirlwind was later struck off charge. Flight Sergeant P.F. Cooper had taken hits to his undercarriage causing it to collapse on landing. Squadron Leader Baker was slightly injured by flying perspex when his canopy took a number of hits...and the ship was not sunk. More attack were made on the ship, the last one on 5 November led by S/L Baker, but 10/10 cloud over the target thwarted the attack. On 10 November 1943, a shipping strike near Guernsey found three ships, which were attacked. A small coaster and two escorting tugs were damaged. That same evening Flying Officer D.W. Sturgeon carried out a night shipping recce. While south-east of Sark he sighted four-five ships. He attacked but no results were seen. A second strike was laid on to attack the same ships. Squadron Leader Bakers bombs exploded alongside a trawler. The following night Flying Officers R.B. Tuff (RAAF) and J.B. Holman were to the West of Guernsey when Flying Officer Tuff sighted two tugs. He attacked and achieved a near miss. Bad weather prevented a number of sorties during the remainder of November. On the 25th and 26th 263 participated to *Ramrod* 106 and 108, an attack on Cherbourg docks. Once more all the Whirwinds suffered flak damages but all could to return base. On the 29th, S/L Baker led three more Whirlwinds to intercept minesweepers or mine destroying Ju52s, thought to be operating off Cherboug. Unfortunately, S/L Baker, F/O Mogg, F/L Snalam and F/O Blakclock found only violent rainstroms and 10/10 cloud. All return to base and when the last Whirlwind touched down at Warmwell, the operational career of the Whirlwind was over. At the end of November 1943, 263 had on charge P6971, P6983, P6990, P6997, P7012, P7037, P7040, P7046, P7055, P7092/D, P7097, P7098, P7100, P7012/N, P7108 and P7111/W, 16 of the 20 Whirlwinds remaining in RAF inventory. By the beginning of December 263 Squadron started to receive Typhoons to replace their Whirlwinds opening a new chapter to 263's history.

Date	Pilot	SN	Origin	Type	Serial	Code	Nb	Cat.
12.01.41	P/O David **Stein**	RAF No. 84299	RAF	Ju88	**P6972**		1.0	C
08.02.41	P/O Kenneth A.G. **Graham**	RAF No. 78737	RAF	Ar196	**P6969**	HE-V	1.0	C
06.08.41	P/O Clifford P. **Rudland***	RAF No. 65998	RAF	Bf109	**P7002**	HE-L	2.0	C
	F/Sgt Robert A. **Brackley**	RAF No. 518164	RAF	Bf109	**P6983**	HE-H	1.0	C
07.11.41	Sgt Cecil P. **King*** *	RAF No. 958932	RAF	Bf109	**P7112**		1.0	C
14.08.43	F/L Ernest R. **Baker*** **	RAF No. 40660	RAF	He111	**P7113**		1.0	C

*in two different sorties

** from West Indies

***Actually a Ju88 from KG 26

Total: 7.0

They didn't make it:
L-R, P/O D.R. Gill (here still wearing his Sergeant stripes, a Canadian from British Columbia, killed on 7 November 1942, Sgt B.C. Abrams, a South Africa serving in the RAF and Sgt E. Brearley, an English-born Canadian whose family had emigrated in Canada in 1927. Both Abrams and Brearley were lost within two days in April 1943. Right, P/O H.J. Blackshaw who was killed one month later on 15 May 1943. He had been awarded the DFC in February 1943 while serving the squadron.
(C. Goss Collection)

Date	Pilot	S/N	Origin	Serial	Code	Fate
29.12.40	F/L Wynford O.L. **Smith**	RAF No. 37366	RAF	**P6975**	HE-L	†
	P/O Donald M. **Vine**	RAF No. 83718	RAF	**P6978**		†
08.02.41	P/O Kenneth A.G. **Graham**	RAF No. 78737	RAF	**P6969**	HE-V	†
11.03.41	P/O Herbert H. **Kitchener**	RAF No. 87029	RAF	**P6985**	HE-J	-
14.03.41	P/O Patrick G. **Thornton-Brown**	RAF No. 81639	RAF	**P6988**		-
01.04.41	F/L David A.C. **Crooks**	RAF No. 40678	(CAN)/RAF	**P6989**	HE-C	†
04.09.41	Sgt Geoffrey L. **Buckwell**	RAF No. 1254477	RAF	**P7042**		**PoW**
10.09.41	P/O Denis W. **Mason**	RAF No. 45726	RAF	**P7001**		†
29.09.41	Sgt Thomas **Hunter**	RAF No. 1001262	RAF	**P7009**		†
30.10.41	F/O David **Stein**	RAF No. 84299	RAF	**P7015**		†
06.11.41	Sgt John J. **Robinson**	RAF No. 1057469	RAF	**P6970**		†
23.07.42	P/O John J. **Walker**	RAF No. 119013	RAF	**P7060**		†
	P/O Vivian L. **Currie**	RAF No. 106035	RAF	**P7035**		†
08.10.42	F/L Arthur N.W. **Johnstone**	RAF No. 42313	RAF	**P7014**	HE-T	-
07.11.42	P/O Donald R. **Gill**	CAN./ J.15111	RCAF	**P7043**	HE-A	†
07.12.42	S/L Robert S. **Woodward**	RAF No. 74698	RAF	**P7105**	HE-N	†
	W/O Donald B. **McPhail**	CAN./ R.67887	RCAF	**P6987**	HE-L	†
12.02.43	Sgt David J. **Williams**	RAF No. 1314587	RAF	**P7052**		†
14.04.43	Sgt John **Macaulay**	RAF No. 1113286	RAF	**P7010**		†
16.04.43	F/O Edgar **Brearley**	CAN./ J.15157	RCAF	**P6995**		†
17.04.43	F/O Philip **Harvey**	RAF No. 102571	(IRE)/RAF	**P7090**		†
	F/O Cecil P. **King***	RAF No. 128999	RAF	**P7117**	HE-H	†
	F/O Basil C. **Abrams**	RAF No. 133547	(SA)/RAF	**P7099**		†
15.05.43	F/L Herbert J. **Blackshaw**	RAF No. 111980	RAF	**P7094**	HE-T	†
22.05.43	F/O Arthur **Lee-White****	RAF No. 121791	RAF	**P7059**		-
23.05.43	P/O Maxwell T. **Cotton**	AUS. 408204	RAAF	**P7089**		-
15.06.43	P/O Maxwell T. **Cotton**	AUS. 408204	RAAF	**P7000**		†
23.09.43	F/Sgt George A. **Wood**	RAF No. 1334647	RAF	**P7113**	HE-W	**Eva.**
08.10.43	P/O James I. **Simpson**	RAF No. 155239	RAF	**P7047**		†
24.10.43	F/O Paul T.R. **Mercer**	RAF No. 127883	RAF	**P6986**	HE-Q	†
	F/Sgt Leonard S. **Gray**	RAF No. 1340994	RAF	**P6979**	HE-G	**PoW**
	F/L David G. **Ross**	RAF No. 84001	RAF	**P6974**	HE-M	-

*from West Indies

**From Peru with British parentage

Total: 32

Date	Pilot	S/N	Origin	Serial	Code	Fate
07.08.40	P/O Irving F. **McDermott**	RAF No. 41719	(CAN)/RAF	**P6966**	HE-X	-
12.12.40	F/O Alan W.N. **Britton**	RAF No. 72033	RAF	**P6980**		†
19.01.41	F/L Thomas P. **Pugh**	RAF No. 40137	RAF	**P6984**	HE-H	-
20.04.41	F/O Bernard **Howe**	RAF No. 33427	RAF	**P6992**	HE-C	†
30.04.41	P/O George S. **Milligan**	RAF No. 87030	RAF	**P7008**		†
29.05.41	Sgt Donald F.J. **Tebbit**	RAF No. 951767	RAF	**P7006**		-
11.06.41	Sgt Reginald G. **Pascoe**	RAF No. 927360	RAF	**L6845**		†
12.06.41	P/O Roy F. **Ferdinand**	RAF No. 80817	RAF	**P7045**		†
15.09.41	*Ground accident*	-	-	**P6996**		-
09.10.41	F/L Humphrey St-J. **Coghlan**	AAF No. 90117	RAF	**P6999**		-
	P/O Ormonde J.H. **Hoskins**	RAF No. 69485	RAF	**P6968**	HE-H	†
14.12.41	Sgt Derrick E. **Prior**	RAF No. 1166018	RAF	**P7044**		†
03.01.42	*Ground accident*	-	-	**P7038**		-
07.03.42	F/Sgt PeterA. **Jardine**	RAF No. 711019	(SA)/RAF	**P7039**		-
14.03.42	P/O Vivian L. **Currie**	RAF No. 106158	RAF	**P7004**		-
01.04.42	P/O Philip **Harvey**	RAF No. 102571	(IRE)/RAF	**P7112**		-
02.04.42	Sgt Basil C. **Abrams**	RAF No. 1377968	(SA)/RAF	**P7041**		-
21.09.42	Sgt Peter A. **Jardine**	RAF No. 711019	(SA)/RAF	**P7003**		†
28.10.42	F/L James R. **Cooksey**	RAF No. 44263	RAF	**P7120**	HE-R	-
09.02.43	Sgt John **Macauley**	RAF No. 1113286	RAF	**P6991**	HE-R	-
19.02.43	F/Sgt Francis L. **Hicks**	Aus. 408207	RAAF	**P7062**	HE-L	†
07.05.43	Sgt John **Thould**	RAF No. 1246400	RAF	**P7057**		-
13.07.43	Sgt Leonard J. **Knott**	raf No. 1386897	RAF	**P7110**	HE-C	-
01.08.43	Sgt Peter F. **Cooper**	RAF No. 1477083	RAF	**P6981**	HE-B	-
10.09.43	S/L Ernest R. **Baker**	RAF No. 40660	RAF	**P7096**		-

Total: 25

P6981/HE-B following Sgt Cooper's crash landing on 1
August 1943...a lucky escape!
(CT Collection)

Serial	date of delivery	Squadron
L6844	24.01.39	**263**
L6845	30.05.40	**25, 263**
P6966	12.06.40	**25, 263** *(HE-Z, HE-X)*
P6967	12.06.40	**25, 263, 137**
P6968	18.07.40	**263** *(HE-H)*
P6969	18.07.40	**263** *HE-V)*
P6970	26.07.40	**263**
P6971	31.08.40	**263, 137, 263**
P6972	01.09.40	**263, 137**
P6973	17.09.40	**263**
P6974	07.09.40	**263** *(HE-Z, HE-M)*
P6975	21.10.40	**263** *(HE-L)*
P6976	07.11.40	**263** *(HE-X)*, **137** *(SF-X)*

Two views of P6976/HE-X after its accident in February 1941. The aircraft was repaired. *(C. Goss Collection)*

P6977	07.11.40	**263, 137**
P6978	12.11.40	**263**
P6979	07.11.40	**263** *(HE-Q, HE-G)*

Germans soldiers inspecting the wreckage of P6979/HE-G in October 1943. It was one of the last operational Whirlwind losses which took place on 24 October during an attack of a vessel in the Cherbourg Harbour. The pilot, F/Sgt L.S. Gray was captured.

Above, P6982/SF-P of 137 Squadron in February 1942. *(CT Collection)*
Below, P6984/HE-H seen at Exeter in the first days of 1941. The aircraft was lost soon after on 19 January when both engines failed, forcing F/L Pugh to bale out.
(Phil Jarrett Collection)

P6980	16.11.40	**263**
P6981	07.10.40	**263** (HE-B), **137** (SF-S), **263**
P6982	26.11.40	**263**, **137** (SF-P, SF-F, SF-S)
P6983	07.10.40	**263** (HE-H), **137**, **263**
P6984	22.12.40	**263** (HE-H)
P6985	03.01.41	**263** (HE-J)
P6986	04.01.41	**263**, **137**, **263** (HE-Q)
P6987	04.01.41	**263** (HE-L)
P6988	04.01.41	**263** (HE-J)
P6989	19.01.41	**263** (HE-J, HE-C)
P6990	19.01.41	**263**
P6991	20.12.40	**263** (HE-R)
P6992	30.12.40	**263** (HE-C)
P6993	30.12.40	**263** (HE-S), **137** (SF-A)
P6994	24.01.41	**263**
P6995	25.02.41	**263**
P6996	24.01.41	**263**
P6997	21.02.41	**263**, **137**, **263**
P6998	24.01.41	**263**, **137**
P6999	24.01.41	**263**
P7000	24.01.41	**263**
P7001	24.01.41	**263**
P7002	13.03.41	**263** (HE-L), **137** (SF-W)
P7003	03.04.41	**263**
P7004	02.03.41	**263**
P7005	24.03.41	**263** (HE-A), **137** (SF-H)
P7006	13.03.41	**263**
P7007	24.03.41	**263**
P7008	04.04.41	**263**
P7009	06.04.41	**263**
P7010	06.04.41	**263**
P7011	10.04.41	**263** (HE-H), **137** (SF-U), **263**

Whirlwind P7011/SF-U seen at Manston at the end of the summer of 1942 (C.T. Collection)

P7012	08.04.41	**137** (SF-V), **263**
P7013	10.04.41	**263**
P7014	10.04.41	**263** (HE-T)
P7015	23.04.41	**263**
P7035	15.04.41	**137**, **263**
P7036	22.04.41	**137** (SF-X)
P7037	28.04.41	**263**, **137** (SF-J), **263**
P7038	27.03.41	**137**, **263**

Above, P7037/SF-J hit a boundary fence on 5 October 1942 without major consequences for both pilot and aircraft.
Below, P7055/SF-S, summer 1942, with the bomb racks under the wings just installed. *(CT Collection - both)*

P7039	30.04.41	**263**
P7040	29.04.41	**263**
P7041	07.05.41	**263**
P7042	12.05.41	**263**
P7043	12.05.41	**263** *(HE-A)*
P7044	03.05.41	**263**
P7045	16.05.41	**263**
P7046	16.05.41	**263, 137, 263**
P7047	22.05.41	**137, 263**
P7048	27.05.41	**137**
P7049	27.05.41	**137**
P7050	24.05.41	**137**
P7051	02.06.41	**263, 137**
P7052	27.02.41	**263**
P7053	12.06.41	**137**
P7054	17.06.41	**137, 263, 137**
P7055	17.06.41	**137** *(SF-S, SF-U)*, **263**
P7056	30.06.41	**263, 137, 263**
P7057	08.06.41	**137** *(SF-S)*, **263**
P7058	22.06.41	**137** *(SF-G)*
P7059	23.06.41	**263**
P7060	23.06.41	**137, 263**
P7061	25.06.41	**263** *(HE-A)*, **137** *(SF-A)*

In the forefront, Whirlwind P7061/HE-A in the autumn of 1941. *(Westland Archives)*

P7062	28.06.41	**263, 137, 263** *(HE-L)*
P7063	27.05.41	**137**
P7064	03.07.41	**137** *(SF-G)*
P7089	02.07.41	**263**
P7090	06.07.41	**137, 263**
P7091	08.07.41	**137**
P7092	06.07.41	**137, 263, 137** *(SF-Q, SF-U)*
P7093	17.07.41	**137** *(SF-A)*

A nice photo of Whirlwind P7062/HE-L in flight in 1942. It was regularly flown by P/O W.A. Lovell, an English-born American serving in the RCAF.

P7094	17.07.41	**137, 263** *(HE-S, HE-T)*
P7095	21.07.41	**137** *(SF-H)*
P7096	24.07.41	**137, 263**
P7097	24.07.41	**137, 263**
P7098	30.07.41	**137** *(SF-P)*, **263**
P7099	30.07.41	**263**
P7100	07.08.41	**263**
P7101	07.08.41	**137** *(SF-A)*
P7102	12.08.41	**137** *(SF-P)*, **263** *(HE-N)*
P7103	18.08.41	**137**
P7104	30.08.41	**137** *(SF-V)*
P7105	30.08.41	**137, 263** *(HE-N)*
P7106	30.08.41	**137** *(SF-D)*
P7107	30.08.41	**137**
P7108	10.09.41	**263**
P7109	10.09.41	**137** *(SF-N)*
P7110	26.09.41	**263** *(HE-E, HE-G, HE-H, HE-C)*
P7111	16.09.41	**137** *(SF-E)*, **263** *(HE-W)*
P7112	26.09.41	**263**
P7113	26.09.41	**263** *(HE-W)*
P7114	29.09.41	**263, 137**
P7115	13.10.41	**137**
P7116	27.10.41	**263** *(HE-F, HE-J, HE-S)*

Above and below, Flying Officer J.P. Coyne (RCAF) of 263 Squadron is posing in P7094/HE-T, probably in April 1943. This aircraft was the F/L H.J. Blackshaw's regular mount and both would be lost a few weeks later, on 15 May 1943. *(Phil Jarrett Collection)*

P7117	27.10.41	**263** (HE-A, HE-G, HE-E, HE-H)
P7118	11.11.41	**137** (SF-O)
P7119	11.11.41	**137** (SF-C, SF-S, SF-W)
P7120	08.12.41	**263** (HE-R, HE -D)
P7121	08.12.41	**137** (SF-C)
P7122	16.12.41	**137**

Sergeant A.E. Brown P7095/SF-H inspected by German officers a few days after he was shot down on 23 January 1943.

IN MEMORIAM

Westland Whirlwind

Name	Service No	Rank	Age	Origin	Date	Serial
ABRAMS, Basil Courtney	RAF No. 133547	F/O	21	(SA)/RAF	18.04.43	P7099
BLACKSHAW, Herbert John	RAF No. 111980	F/L	26	RAF	16.05.43	P7094
BREARLEY, Edgar	CAN./ J.15157	F/O	26	RCAF	17.04.43	P6995
BRENNAN, John Robert	CAN./ R.72637	F/Sgt	19	RCAF	27.05.42	P7122
BRITTON, Allan Walter Nayler	RAF No. 72033	F/O	23	RAF	12.12.40	P6980
BROWN, Alfred Edward	RAF No. 141474	P/O	27	RAF	23.01.43	P7095
CLARCK, Colin Anthony Gordon	RAF No. 42192	F/O	28	(SA)/RAF	30.10.41	P7091
COTTON, Maxwell Tylney	AUS. 408204	P/O	22	RAAF	15.06.43	P7000
CROOKS, David Alexander Cummings	RAF No. 40678	F/L	28	(CAN)/RAF	01.04.41	P6989
CURRIE, Vivian Lester	RAF No. 106035	P/O	22	RAF	23.07.42	P7035
DE-SHANE, Charles Wilbert	CAN./ J.15148	P/O	20	RCAF	09.03.42	P7036
FERDINAND, Roy Frederick	RAF No. 80817	P/O	21	RAF	12.06.41	P7045
FREEMAN, Neville Austin	SAAF No. 19862	Lt	21	SAAF	18.02.43	P7119
GILL, Donald Ross	CAN./ J.15111	F/O	27	RCAF	07.11.42	P7043
GRAHAM, Kenneth Alfred George	RAF No. 78737	P/O	20	RAF	08.02.41	P6969
HADOW, John Maude	RAF No. 122121	F/O	20	RAF	16.04.43	P7121
HÄGGBERG, Ralph Otto Gustav	RAF No. 120677	P/O	19	(SWE)/RAF	12.02.42	P7093
HARVEY, Philip	RAF No. 102574	F/O	23	(IRE)/RAF	18.04.43	P7090
HICKS, Francis Leslie	AUS. 408207	F/Sgt	30	RAAF	19.02.43	P7062
HOSKINS, Ormonde John Horace	RAF No. 69485	P/O	26	RAF	09.10.41	P6968
HOWE, Bernard	RAF No. 33427	F/O	22	RAF	20.04.41	P6992
HUNTER, Thomas	RAF No. 1001262	Sgt	21	RAF	29.09.41	P7009
JARDINE, Peter Alastair	RAF No. 711019	Sgt	20	(SA)/RAF	21.09.42	P7003
JOWITT, Douglas St.John	RAF No. 114169	P/O	23	RAF	28.10.42	P7115
KING, Cecil Percy*	RAF No. 128999	F/O	23	RAF	17.04.43	P7117
MACAULEY, John	RAF No. 1113286	Sgt	23	RAF	14.04.43	P7010
MARTIN, George William	RAF No. 102619	P/O	n/k	RAF	12.02.42	P7106
MASON, Dennis William	RAF No. 45726	P/O	23	RAF	10.09.41	P7001
McPHAIL, Donald Burton	CAN./ R.67887	W/O	25	RCAF	07.12.42	P6987
MERCER, Charles Eldred	CAN./ J.15738	P/O	24	RCAF	18.02.43	P7114
MERCER, Paul Thomas Richard	RAF No. 127883	F/O	n/k	RAF	24.10.43	P6986
MILLIGAN, George Stanley	RAF No. 87030	P/O	22	RAF	30.04.41	P7008
MUSGRAVE, Edward Lancelot	AUS. 403528	F/O	25	RAAF	18.05.43	P7063
PASCOE, Reginald Gunn	RAF No. 927360	Sgt	20	RAF	11.06.41	L6845
PRIOR, Derrick Ellis	RAF No. 1166018	Sgt	21	RAF	14.12.41	P7044
REBBETOY, James Reginald	CAN./ J.15741	F/O	26	RCAF	25.04.43	P7058
ROBERTSON, Basil Lionell	RAF No. 748333	W/O	20	RAF	12.02.42	P7107
ROBINSON, John Joseph	RAF No. 1057469	Sgt	21	RAF	06.11.41	P6970
SAMPLE, John	AAF No. 90278	S/L	28	RAF	28.10.41	P7053
SANDY, John Anthony William	RAF No. 116508	P/O	n/k	RAF	12.02.42	P7050
SIMPSON, James Ian	RAF No. 155239	P/O	24	RAF	08.10.43	P7047
SMITH, Wynford Ormonde Leoni	RAF No. 37366	F/L	25	RAF	29.12.40	P6978
VINE, Donald Martin	RAF No. 83718	P/O	23	RAF	29.12.40	P6975

*From the West Indies

Walker, John James	RAF No. 119013	P/O	22	RAF	23.07.42	P7060
Williams, David John	RAF No. 1314587	Sgt	20	RAF	12.02.43	P7052
Woodward, Robert Sinckler	RAF No. 74698	S/L	23	RAF	07.12.42	P7105
Wright, Robert Elmer Douglas	Can./ J.15147	P/O	26	RCAF	04.05.42	P7103

Total: 47

Australia: 1, Canada: 9, Ireland: 1, South Africa: 4, Sweden: 1, United Kingdom: 31

n/k: Not known

Pilots of 263 enjoying a cup of tea.
Seated: Sgt B.C. Abrames, South Africa (†18.04.43), P/O J.J. Walker (†23.07.42), F/Sgt H.D. Muirhead (RCAF, †17.02.43 with 401 Sqn), F/Sgt C.P. King (West Indies, †17.04.43), Sgt K.C. Ridley, Sgt J.E. Meredith.
Standing: P/O H.J. Blackshaw (†15.05.43)S/L R.S. Woodward (CO, †07.12.42)F/L G.B. Warnes (†22.02.44 as OC); P/O N.V. Crabtree (American serving in the RCAF, †10.11.44 with the USAAF), P/O J.W.E. Holmes, F/L E.C. Owens (Adj), F/L C.P. Rudland, P/O A.S. Wordsworth (IO), P/O A.A. Hay (EO), P/O P. Harvey (Irish, †15.04.43), P/O V.L. Currie (†23.07.42)
(C. Goss Collection)

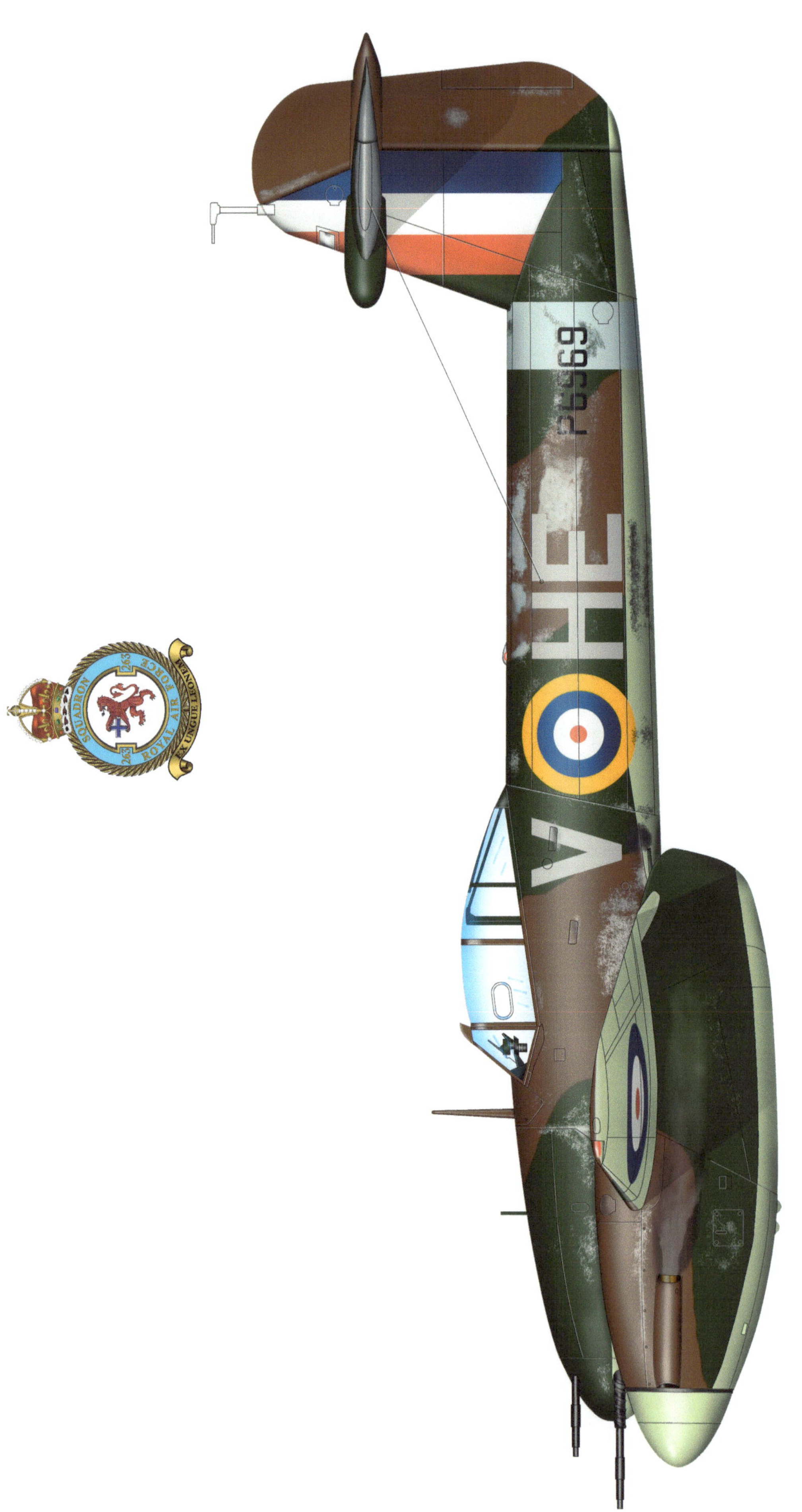

Westland Whirlwind Mk. I P6969
No. 263 Squadron
Exeter (UK), Autumn 1940

Westland Whirlwind Mk. I P6987
No. 263 Squadron
Exeter (UK), Spring 1941

Westland Whirlwind Mk. I P7061
No. 263 Squadron
Charmy Down (UK), Autumn 1941

Thomas Patrick PUGH

RAF No. 40137

Thomas Pugh joined the RAF on a Short Service Commission in July 1937. Upon completion of his training he was posted as a Fairey Battle pilot with No. 103 Squadron. He followed his unit to France as part of the AASF. Returning to the UK, he was re-trained as a fighter pilot and in, July 1940, was posted to No. 263 Squadron. In September, he was commanding B Flight and in August 1941 he was given command of the squadron and would lead it until the end of his tour in February 1942. He left with a DFC ribbon awarded in October 1941.

Serving as Squadron Leader Tactics, HQ 82 Group, he was subsequently posted, in September 1942, as OC to No. 182 Squadron, then under formation, after having gained some experience on Typhoons with Nos. 56 and 266 (Southern Rhodesia) Squadrons. He led the unit until being killed in action on 2 August when he was shot down by flak in his Typhoon while attacking a destroyer in Dunkirk harbour.

A well known photograph taken in 1942 at the time S/L T.P. Pugh was 263's CO. At the end of his tour, he used to fly P7116/HE-F 'Bellows Argentina No 2'. This aircraft is one of the Whirlwinds which were funded by the Fellowship of the Bellows in Argentina and in Uruguay.

Westland Whirlwind Mk. I P7116
No. 263 Squadron
Squadron Leader Thomas T. PUGH
Colerne (UK), January-February 1942

Westland Whirlwind Mk. I P6982
No. 137 Squadron
Matlask (UK), February 1942

Westland Whirlwind Mk. I P7062
No. 263 Squadron
Angle (UK), July 1942

Westland Whirlwind Mk. I P7043
No. 263 Squadron
Flight Lieutenant Geoffrey B. WARNES
Warmwell (UK), Autumn 1942

Westland Whirlwind Mk. I P7037
No. 137 Squadron
Manston (UK), October 1942

Westland Whirlwind Mk. I P7092

No. 137 Squadron
Manston (UK), Spring 1943

Westland Whirlwind Mk. I P7094

No. 263 Squadron
Flight Lieutenant Herbert J. BLACKSHAW
Warmwell (UK), May 1943

Westland Whirlwind Mk. I P7111
No. 137 Squadron
Matlask (UK), Summer 1942

Westland Whirlwind Mk. I P7111
No. 263 Squadron
Warmwell (UK), Summer 1943

SQUADRONS! - The series

SQUADRONS!
No.54
Phil H. LISTEMANN
The Hawker
Biplane Fighters

No.137 Squadron
1941 - 1945
COMPILED BY
H. LISTEMANN
WITH
CHRIS THOMAS

USN AIRCRAFT
1922-1962
Vol.7:
Designation Letter
'F' (Pt-4)

James Edgar JOHNSON DSO** DFC*
Supermarine Spitfire Mk.XIV MV257
No. 125 Wing
Group Captain J. E. Johnson
RAF No. 83267
B.160/Kastrup (Denmark), June 1945

www.RAF-IN-COMBAT.com

- USN Aircraft 1922-1962 -
- Squadrons! -
- RAF, Dominion and Allied squadrons at War -
- Allied Wings -
- Fighter Leaders -
- Prints (Aces and Leaders) -

Fighter Leaders
of the RAF, RAAF, RCAF, RNZAF & SAAF in WW2
Volume VII
Phil H. Listemann

ALLIED WINGS
No.19
The English Electric CANBERRA
B(I).8
Phil. H. LISTEMANN

SQUADRONS!
No.17
Phil H. LISTE
The Curtiss
Mohawk